How Big? Animals

By Lisa Regan and Patrick Corrigan

ARCTURUS

ARCTURUS

First edition published in 2024 by Arcturus Publishing Limited
26/27 Bickels Yard, 151–153 Bermondsey Street,
London SE1 3HA

Author: Lisa Regan
Illustrator: Patrick Corrigan
Editor: Violet Peto
Consultant: Anne Rooney
Designer: Simon Oliver
Managing Editor: Joe Harris
Managing Designer: Georgina Wood

Published and Distributed in India by Scholastic India Pvt. Ltd.
First edition: 2024
This reprint edition: July 2024
ISBN: 978-93-5954-548-6
Printed in India at Polykam Offset New Delhi 110028

Contents

How Big?

Everyone knows that an elephant is big, but can you picture just ***how*** big? This book will help you to size up a whole range of different animals. We'll use metric and imperial units of measurement and real-life comparisons. And to really bring things home, we'll also show some animals—or parts of them—at actual size on the page.

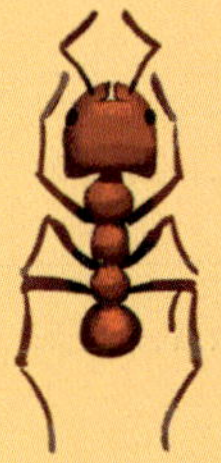

The long and short of it

How long is a toucan's beak? Or a tiger's tail? You could make a guess just by looking at them. In the case of the toucan's beak, you could look at the cover of this book! Or you could measure them.

Length is measured in metric units (cm, m) or imperial units (in, ft). So we might say that a tiger's tail is up to 110 cm long—or we could say it's 3.6 ft long.

Sometimes, it's easier to picture how long something is by comparing it to other items. For example—the rhinoceros beetle on page 8 measures around 18 cm (7 in), and that's about as long as a pencil.

Weighing things up

Size isn't just about length and height. To get an idea of an animal's physical presence, we need to think about weight, too.

We can use measurements to get a sense of an animal's weight. Weight is measured in grams and kilograms (g, kg) or ounces and pounds (oz, lb). You might say that a fully grown white rhino weighs up to 3,600 kg (8,000 lb).

Another option would be to use a comparison. So for example, you could say that a white rhino weighs as much as a traffic helicopter!

Or try this one for size. A large tarantula weighs roughly 150 g (5 oz)—which is about the same as an apple.

Ready, set ...

How do we describe animals in action? We might want to get a sense of how fast they move. To calculate their speed, we measure how far they can move in a certain amount of time. Most speeds are measured in km/h (km per hour) or mph (miles per hour). However, for very slow animals, it's better to use cm/second or ft/second.

Actual Size

How Big is a Giraffe?

Giraffes are the tallest animals on our planet. They use their long neck to reach the leaves on trees, and they can run at more than 60 km/h (37 mph) on their long legs.

A giraffe's neck is 18 times as long as a human's, but they both have the same number of neck bones! A giraffe's seven neck bones are just much, much bigger.

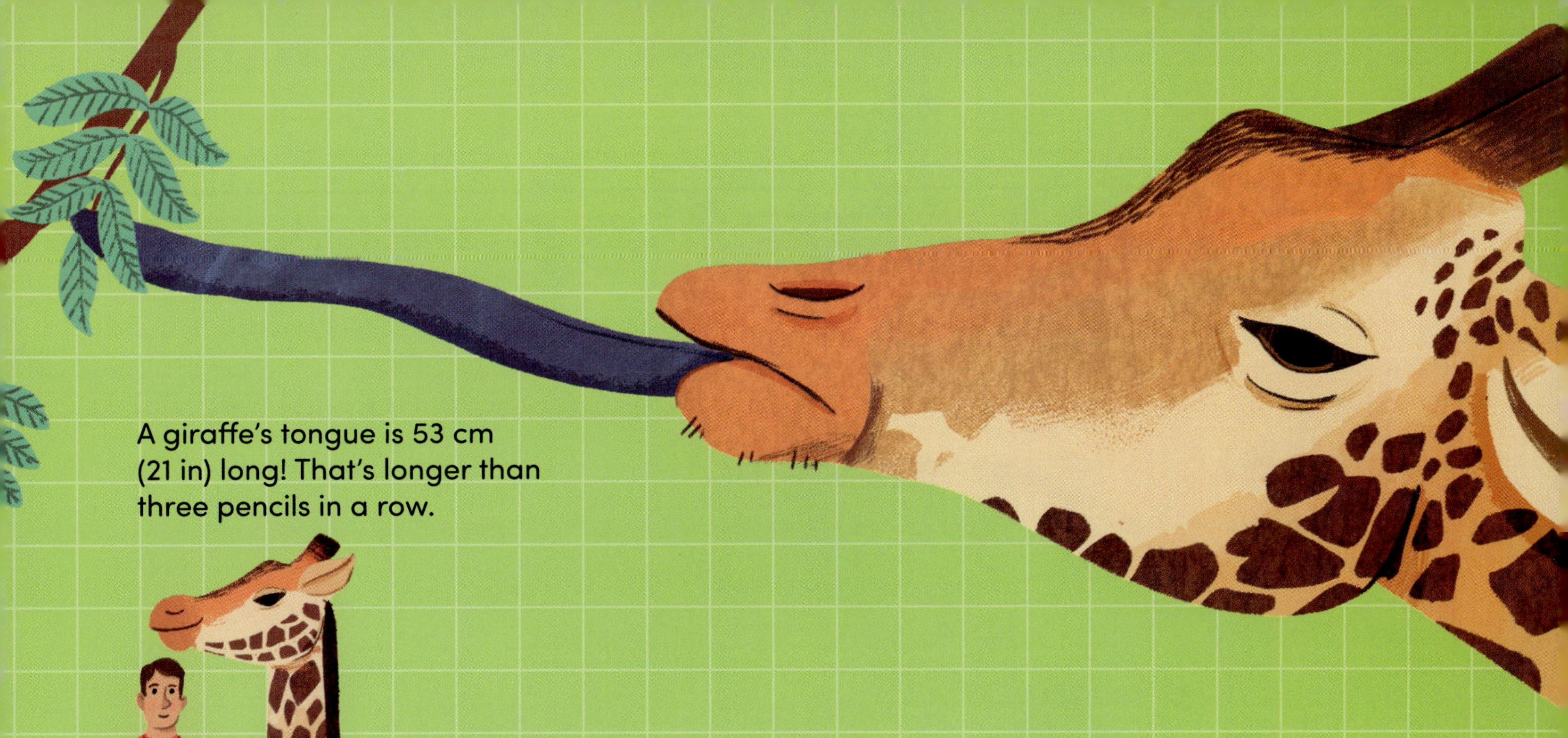

A giraffe's tongue is 53 cm (21 in) long! That's longer than three pencils in a row.

If three adults stood on each other's shoulders, they would be almost as tall as a giraffe.

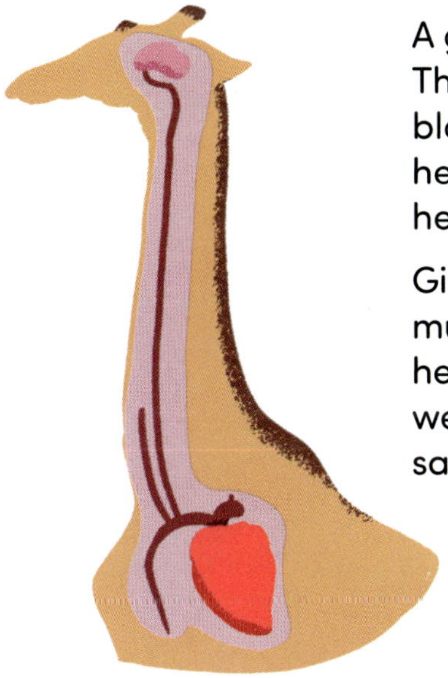

A giraffe has a big heart. That's because it has to pump blood all the way up to its head—1.8 m (6 ft) up! That's the height of a Christmas tree.

Giraffe hearts have strong muscles, which make them heavy too. A giraffe heart weighs 11 kg (24 lb), or about the same as a medium-sized dog.

How do we compare?

	Human	**Male giraffe**
Height	1.7 m (5.6 ft)	6 m (20 ft)
Neck Length	10 cm (4 in)	1.8 m (6 ft)
Leg Length	76 cm (2.5 ft)	1.8 m (6 ft)

How Big is the Biggest Beetle?

The largest beetle in the world is the Titan beetle. Like all beetles, its body is divided into three sections, and it has six legs.

Actual Size

A Titan beetle has biting mouthparts called mandibles. They are sharp enough to bite through human skin or snap a tree branch or pencil in two!

Some of the largest beetles in the world belong to the rhinoceros beetle subfamily. They get their name from the giant horn on the front of their head.

Rhinoceros beetles are very strong for their body size. They can carry 30 times their own weight—the same as a person carrying an actual rhinoceros!

This is a Hercules beetle (a type of rhinoceros beetle). Its horn is 10 cm (4 in) long, the length of a highlighter pen!

How Big Is a Rhino's Ear?

A rhino's ear is not all that large compared to its head size. Look at this ear, then the picture on the opposite page. Now imagine how big its whole body must be!

This rhinoceros has a hitchhiker—a bird called an oxpecker.

Actual Size

There are two types of rhino in Africa: the white rhino and the black rhino. The white rhino is the bigger of the two and has a wide, square mouth.

This rhino has two horns, a long one and a short one. Its long horn can grow to over 1.5 m (5 ft)–that's longer than a bathtub!

A fully grown white rhino can be over 3 m (10 ft) long from head to toe, and weigh up to 3,600 kg (8,000 lb). That's about the length of a row boat and the weight of a traffic helicopter!

Rhinos may be big, but they are not slow. They can reach speeds up to 55 km/h (34 mph), which is faster than your car as you drive past a school!

How does an adult human measure up against a rhino?

How Big Are a Crocodile's Teeth?

These teeth belong to the biggest crocodile on the planet—the saltwater crocodile. Its longest teeth can grow up to 10 cm (4 in), including the root.

Crocodiles lose and regrow teeth frequently—they can get through about 8,000 in their lifetime!

The saltwater crocodile lives in northern Australia and parts of Asia. It can live in fresh water or swim far out into the ocean.

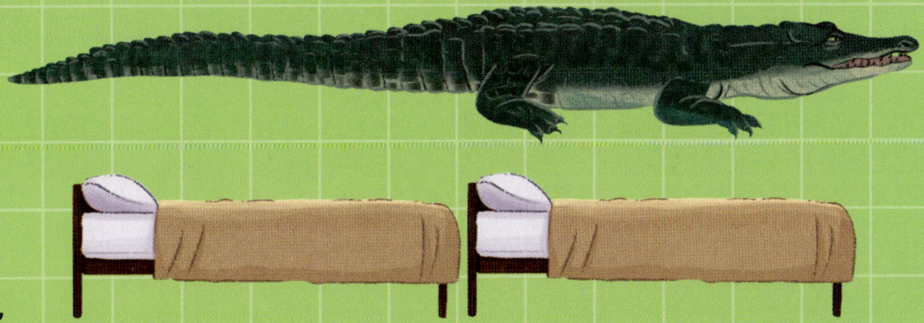

The saltwater crocodile is the world's largest reptile. From nose to tail, it measures at least 5 m (16.4 ft)—longer than two beds end to end.

A crocodile's eyes, ears, and nostrils are on top of its head. It can hide almost completely underwater and still see, hear, and breathe.

Crocodiles are reptiles, and so their babies hatch from eggs. The female lays up to 60 eggs on the river bank.

After around 90 days, the babies appear. Each one is tiny compared to its parents—smaller than a person's forearm. The mother carefully carries them to the water in her mouth.

How Big Is a Gorilla's Hand?

Gorillas and humans are both primates, so their bodies are similar in lots of ways. Both have hands with four fingers and a thumb, and feet with five toes.

A gorilla's hand is huge—two or three times the size of your hand. Their hands are hairy on the back, but they have smooth palms just like you.

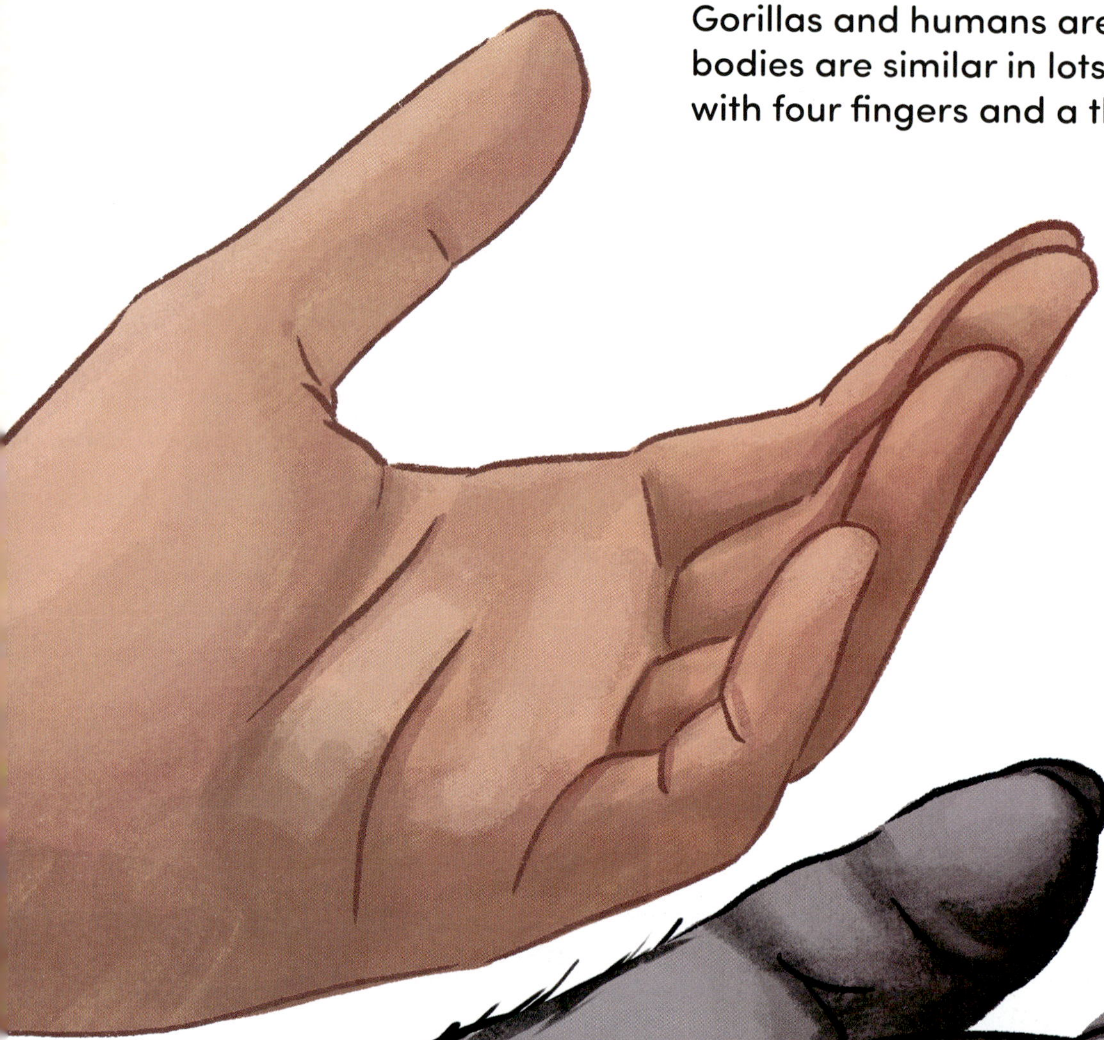

Actual Size

Gorillas have a big ridge above their eyes, called the brow ridge. It helps to make their skull stronger for crushing tough food such as nuts.

A human's armspan is usually the same as their height, while a gorilla's is much, much bigger.

One of the most impressive things about a gorilla is its long arms. Spread wide, they are up to 2.5 m (8 ft)—as long as a surfboard!

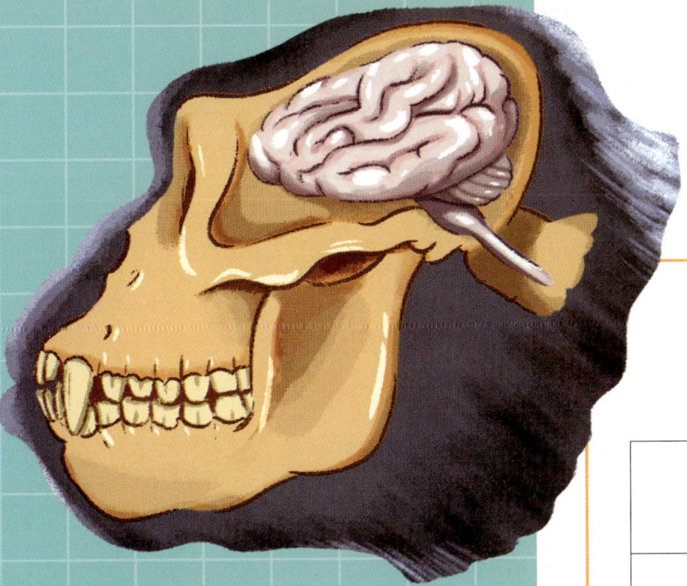

A gorilla's head is bigger than the head of a human, but its brain is smaller. A gorilla's brain is only about one third the size of a human's.

How do we compare?

	Human	Male gorilla
Height	1.7 m (5.6 ft)	1.5 m (5 ft)
Weight	90 kg (200 lb)	170kg (375 lb)
Arm span	1.7 m (5.6 ft)	2.5 m (8 ft)
Brain	1300 g (2.8 lb)	500 g (1 lb)

A gorilla is as tall as a man, if both stand upright.

How Small Is a Hummingbird?

There are over 350 species of hummingbird, all of them found in the Americas. The smallest of them all is Cuba's bee hummingbird, which is only 5 cm (1.9 in) long.

Actual Size

This tiny bird weighs less than a small coin—only around 2 g (0.07 oz).

A hummingbird's large heart can beat more than 20 times per second—that's over 1,200 beats per minute!

Hummingbirds flap their wings incredibly fast so they can hover in midair. They have strong chest muscles and shoulder bones that can move their wings in a figure of eight pattern.

A tiny bird makes a tiny nest and lays tiny eggs. The eggs of the bee hummingbird are the size of a raisin!

Many hummingbirds are bigger than the bee hummingbird. The sword-billed hummingbird has a body around 10 cm (4 in) long, and a beak that is longer than its body!

How Small Is a Jerboa?

There are more than 30 species of jerboa and they are all small—no bigger than a phone. They are famous for their huge feet and very, very long tail.

Actual Size

These tiny creatures hunt at night for insects and grubs. They also eat seeds and roots. A jerboa has huge eyes and long whiskers to help it find its way in the dark.

In some species, their tail can be twice as long as their head and body. Jerboas live in the desert and burrow underground to escape from the hot days and cold nights.

A jerboa has back legs like a miniature kangaroo. They can jump as high as the height of a human and as far as the length of a kayak!

How does a jerboa measure up to a lightbulb?

The long-eared jerboa has ears bigger than its head. Its ears can be two or three times as long as its body. That's like a tall human having 122-cm- (4-ft-) long ears!

How Big Is a Butterfly?

Butterflies come in lots of sizes, and even different shapes. The smallest ones would only just cover your thumbnail. One of the biggest is this blue morpho butterfly, which is as big as a paper party plate.

Actual Size

The blue morpho butterfly can be found in the rain forests of Central and South America. Its wings flash blue because of the way the light reflects off tiny scales.

Butterflies drink through a long mouthpart called a proboscis. It unrolls so they can sip fruit juice, tree sap, or nectar from flowers.

The Queen Alexandra's birdwing is the largest butterfly in the world. Females are bigger than males, but their wings aren't as brightly patterned.

Some butterflies migrate to find warmer weather for the winter. Monarch butterflies like these travel thousands of miles from Canada and the US to Mexico.

Tens of thousands of monarch butterflies gather on trees in the Mexican mountains. They can weigh so much together that their weight breaks off branches.

The Queen Alexandra's birdwing's wingspan can be up to 28 cm (11 inches) across—that's as long as an American football.

How Loud Is a **Lion?**

VERY loud! A lion's mighty roar can be heard up to 8 km (5 miles) away.

A lion can open its mouth extremely wide, revealing its giant teeth. Its long canines are 7 cm (2.75 in)—longer than your finger!

Lions often hunt and feed at night, when it is cooler, and sleep during the hot African daytime. They can snooze for up to 20 hours every day!

A lion's pawprint has four toes, but its claws don't show. The lion pulls its claws in when it walks to protect them.

When they aren't pulled in, a lion's claws can be 3.8 cm (1.5 in) long.

A lion weighs a lot more than a lioness. A large male can easily weigh as much as 50 pet cats!

How do we compare?

	Human	Male lion
Height	1.7 m (5.6 ft)	1.2 m (4 ft)
Weight	90 kg (200 lb)	190 kg (420 lb)
Body Length	1.7 m (5.6 ft)	2 m (6.5 ft)
Tail Length	Zero!	Up to 1 m (3.25 ft)

How Long Is a Monkey's Tail?

This is a spider monkey. It lives in tropical rain forests in Mexico and South America. Its tail is extreeeeeeemely long—longer than its body!

The end of its tail is prehensile. That means it can curl round and grab on to things, such as tree branches. That leaves its hands free for climbing or holding food.

A spider monkey's front feet, or hands, act like hooks to help it swing quickly through the treetops.

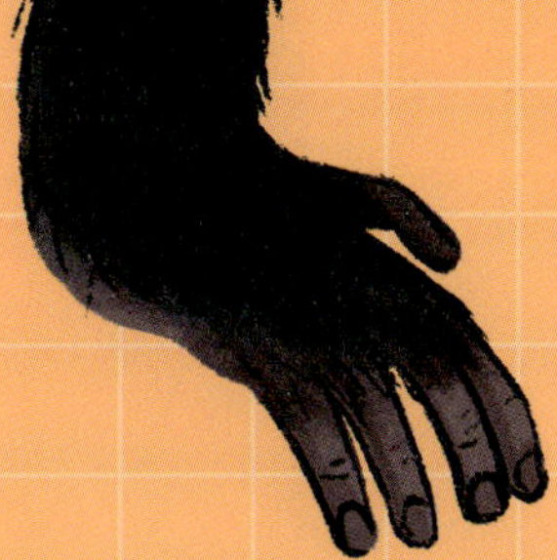

Each foot has a prehensile big toe that can also bend and grip to help it hold on in the trees.

A spider monkey's arms and legs are also exceptionally long. It is these long limbs that give it its name.

The tail is strong enough to support the monkey's whole body weight. That's up to 9 kg (almost 20 lb)—the weight of a bowling ball.

How Big Is a Toucan's Beak?

This beak is awesome! It measures up to 19 cm (8 in), which is a third of the toucan's body length.

A toucan's beak has serrated edges, like a bread knife. It helps the bird to eat. A toucan's diet is mostly fruit, although toucans sometimes eat eggs and insects, too.

Actual Size

The bird's thin, flat tongue is 15 cm (6 in) long, so nearly as long as its beak. Its tongue has a frayed tip.

Toco toucans live in South America. They make their nest inside a tree trunk, climbing in and out through a small hole.

A toucan uses its long beak for reaching fruit on the very ends of thin branches. Its feet have two toes facing forward and two toes facing backward, to help it hold on tightly.

There are lots of different species of toucan. Some are only the size of a crow. The toco toucan is the biggest species with the longest beak.

How Huge Is a Hornet?

A hornet is a type of wasp, and the largest hornets are found in Asia. They live in a nest with a huge queen and thousands of slightly smaller female workers.

They make their hive in a hollow tree, or underground in an abandoned burrow. The queen lays her eggs inside, and the workers look after them and find food.

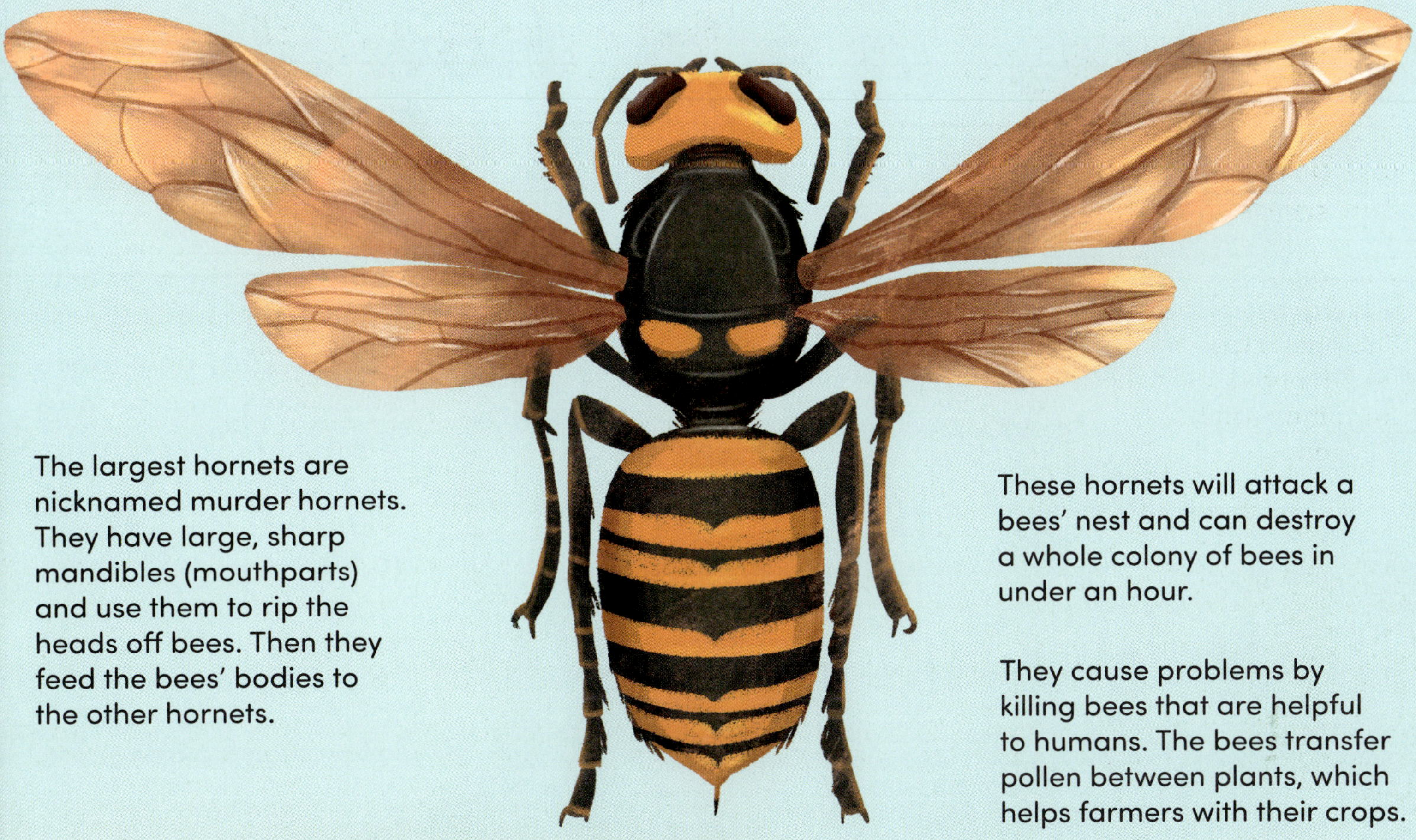

The largest hornets are nicknamed murder hornets. They have large, sharp mandibles (mouthparts) and use them to rip the heads off bees. Then they feed the bees' bodies to the other hornets.

These hornets will attack a bees' nest and can destroy a whole colony of bees in under an hour.

They cause problems by killing bees that are helpful to humans. The bees transfer pollen between plants, which helps farmers with their crops.

How does a murder hornet measure up to a paperclip?

The two large teardrop shapes on its head are eyes. It also has three small, round eyes called ocelli, which can sense light and dark.

How Slow Is a Sloth?

Sloths are the slowest mammals on the planet! They only move when they have to, and even then, they crawl at a top speed of 3 cm/second (0.1 ft/second).

The claws of a three-toed sloth are an awesome 10 cm (4 in) long—slightly longer than a playing card.

Most mammals have seven bones in their neck, but three-toed sloths have up to three extra. This means they can turn their head nearly all the way around.

They move slowly to save energy, and even their insides work slowly. Sloths generally eat tough leaves, and it can take two weeks to digest their food.

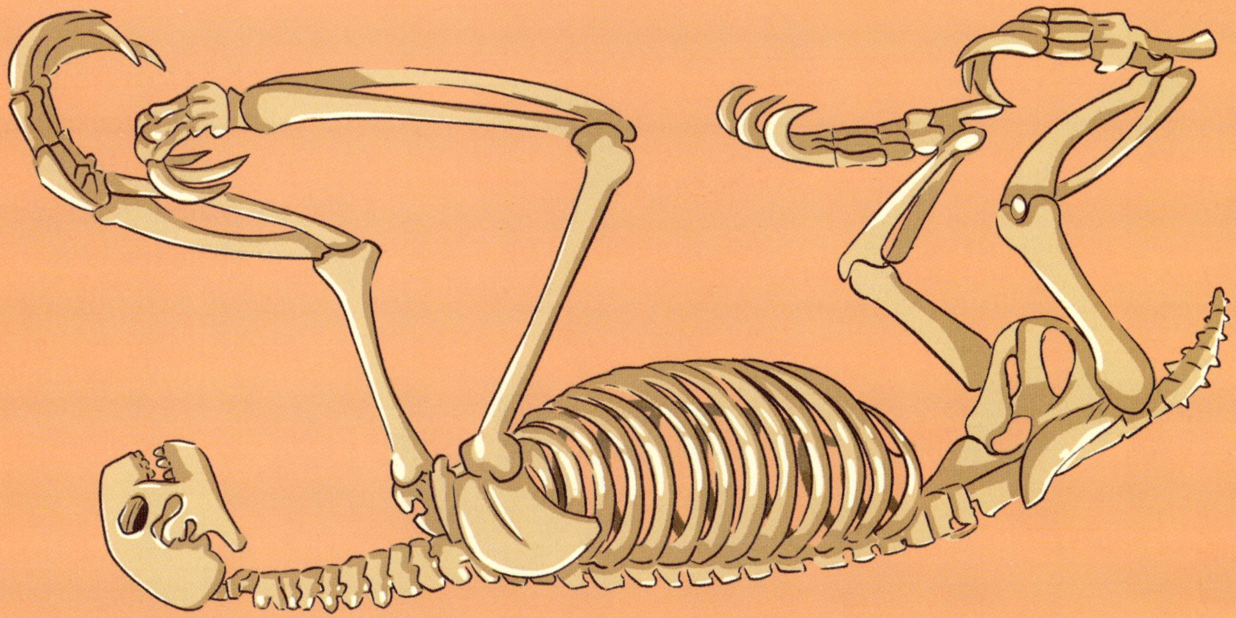

An adult three-toed sloth is the size of a large cat.

Three-toed sloths have long arms and shaggy fur that sometimes looks green because of algae growing in it.

If a sloth looks like it is smiling, the chances are it's a three-toed sloth. Their facial markings look like a permanent grin!

How Big Is a Cheetah?

A cheetah has a long, slim body and a small head. It is built for sprinting and is the world's fastest land animal. Its body is up to 1.5 m (5 ft) long.

Actual Size

The dark lines underneath its eyes help it to hunt in the daytime. They stop the bright sun from glaring into the animal's eyes so it can see its prey better.

Cheetahs can run as fast as a car on a highway, but only for a short time. If they don't catch their prey quickly, they have to stop and rest.

How do we compare?

	Human	Male cheetah
Height	1.7 m (5.6 ft)	0.9 m (3 ft)
Weight	90 kg (200 lb)	65 kg (143 lb)
Tail Length	none!	0.75 m (2.5 ft)
Top speed*	32 km/h (20 mph)*	113 km/h (70 mph)

*This is the speed of an Olympic sprinter, not an ordinary person!

A cheetah's tail is about half as long as its body. It measures between 60 and 75 cm (2—2.3 ft). This long tail helps the cheetah to balance and change direction at top speed.

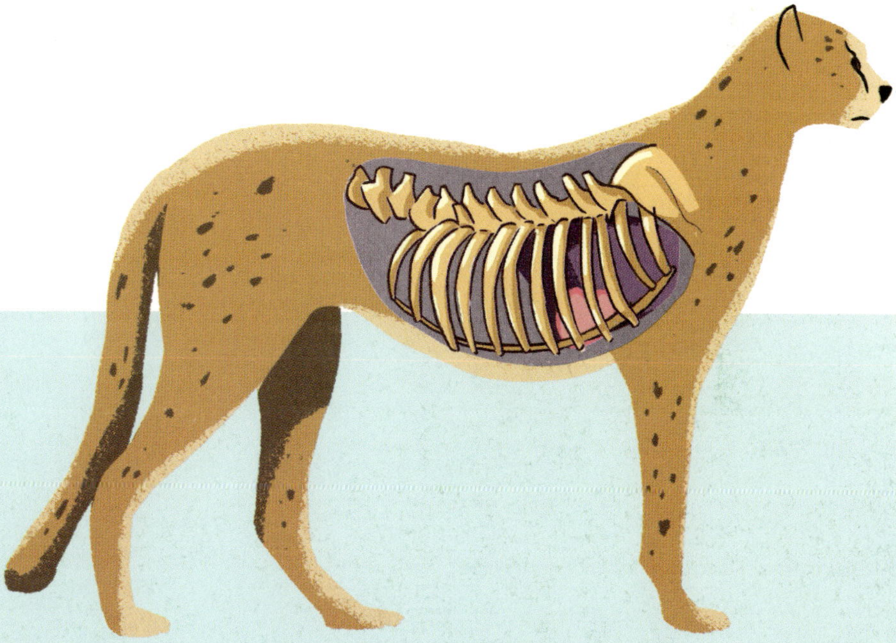

To help it run fast, a cheetah has a huge heart for its size. Its lungs and blood vessels are also exceptionally large.

Actual Size

How Big Are an Orca's Teeth?

An orca is a type of toothed whale in the dolphin family. Its teeth are pointed and large. Some are ten times longer than a human tooth.

Its teeth are used for ripping and tearing, but not for chewing. Some orcas have 40 teeth, while others have as many as 56.

An orca has the largest brain of all dolphins. It weighs around 7 kg (15 lb)—that's around four times heavier than a human brain.

The orca's tail fins are called flukes. They have no bones inside. The orca swims using large muscles in front of the flukes to move its body up and down.

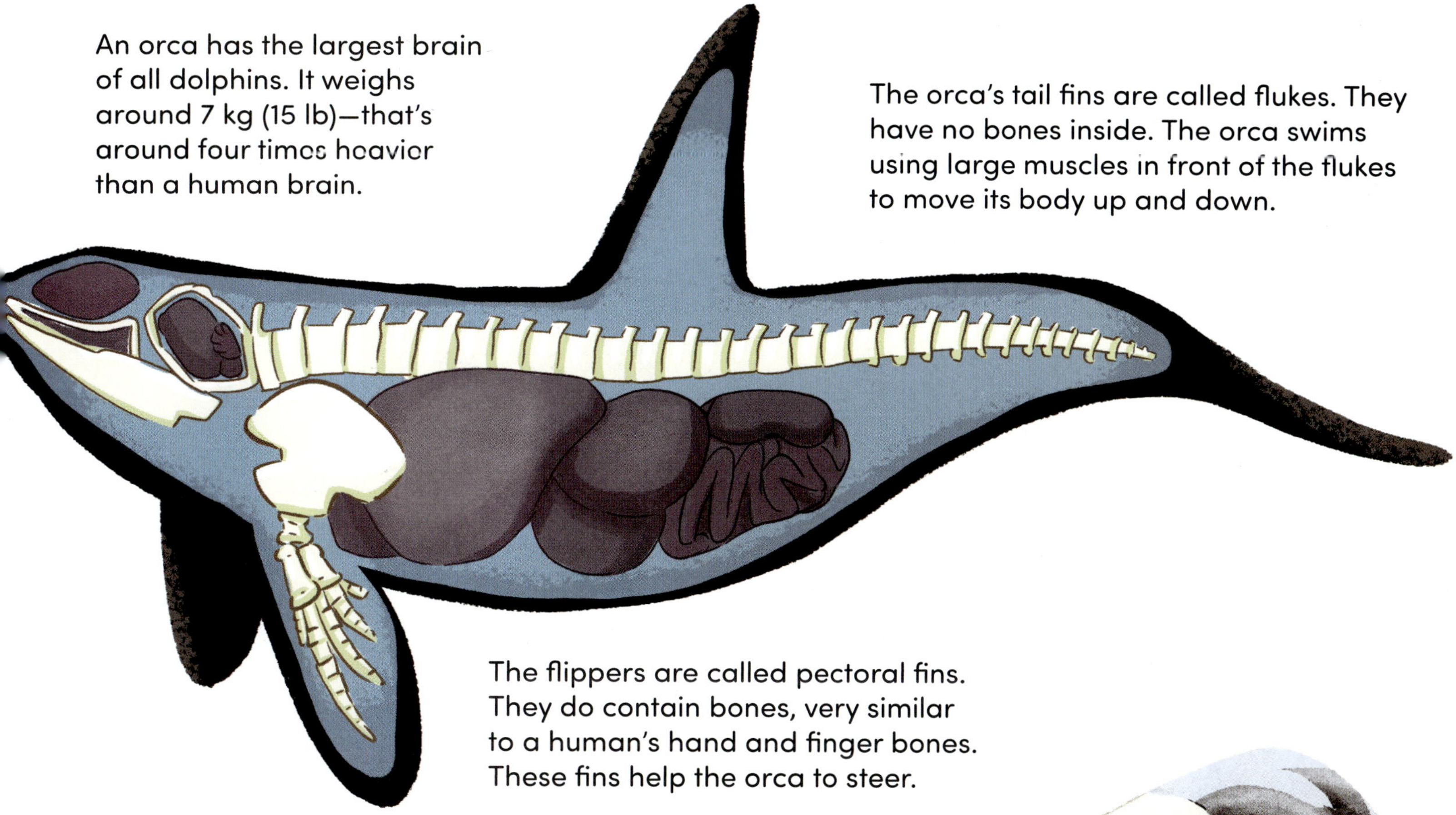

The flippers are called pectoral fins. They do contain bones, very similar to a human's hand and finger bones. These fins help the orca to steer.

Males are bigger than females, and their dorsal (back) fin is bigger, too. It can be 1.8 m (6 ft) tall—the size of a tall man.

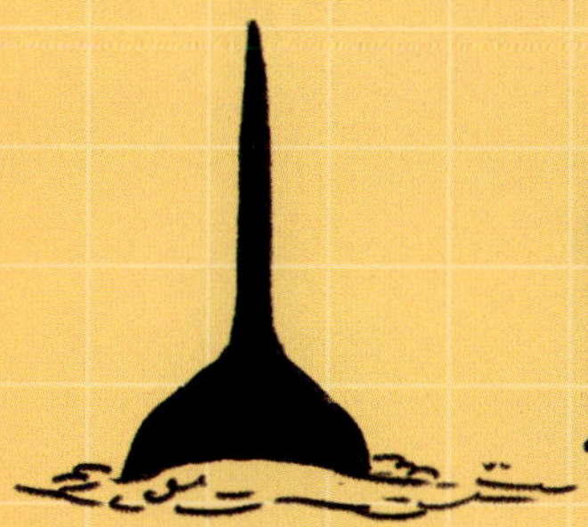

An adult orca can weigh up to six tons. Despite that, they can leap out of the water in a move known as breaching.

How Big Is the Biggest Snail?

The world's largest snail is the giant African land snail. It is big enough to fill the palm of a grown man's hand.

These snails reach their giant size because they never stop growing! They can live for ten years, and will grow until they die.

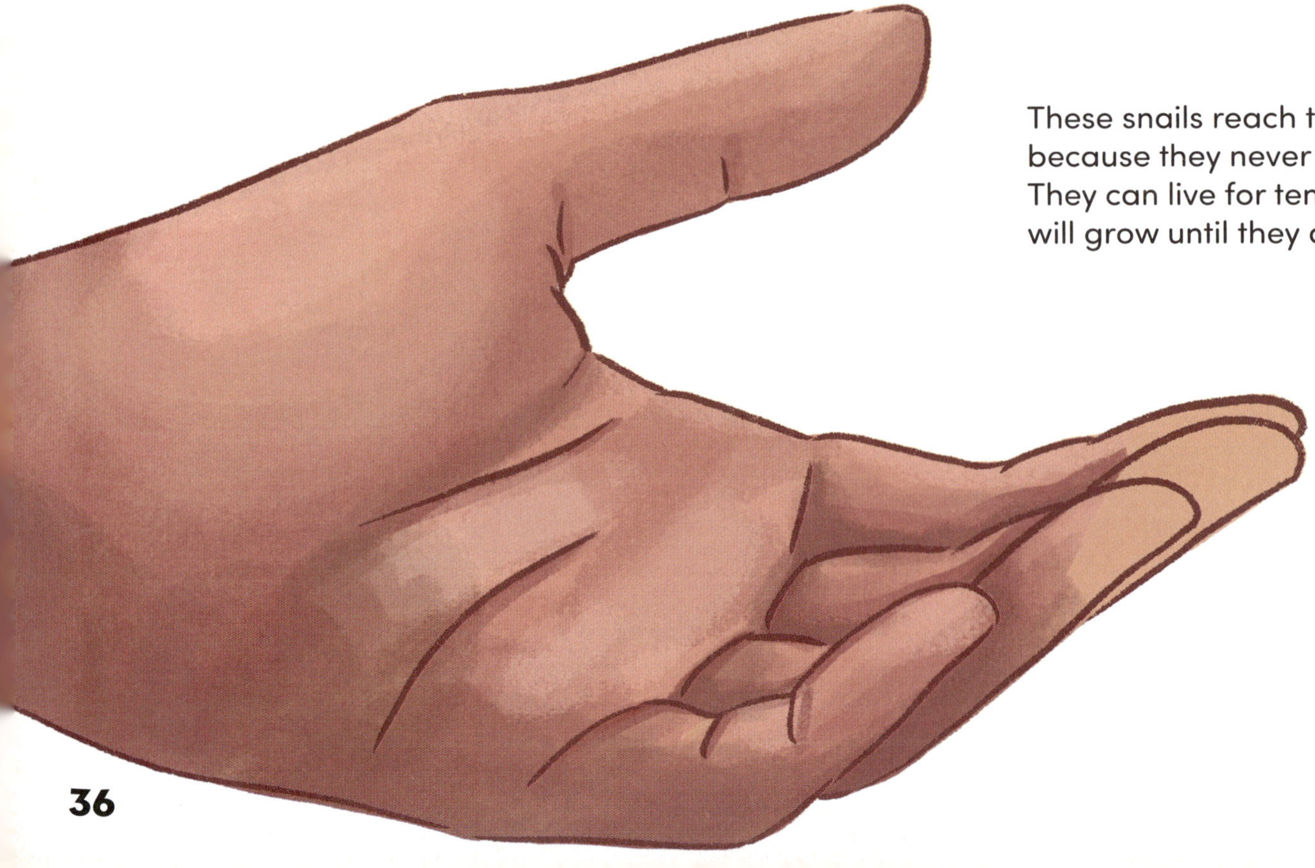

A snail's shell is made of calcium carbonate. More rings are added in a spiral as the snail grows. You can tell the rough age of the snail by counting its rings.

Snails are a type of creature called a gastropod. They move along using a strong, muscular foot under their body.

When they move, snails leave a shiny trail of slime. This special gel helps them glide, stick to walls, and protects their delicate body.

Here's how a giant African land snail measures up to a human hand.

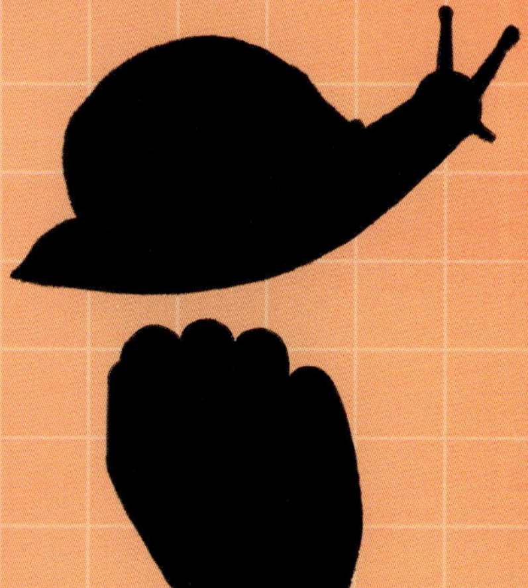

They have two sets of tentacles. The shorter ones are for smelling, and the longer ones have eyes on the ends.

How Big Is a Tiger's Paw?

There are several species of tiger. The largest is the Siberian tiger. Its paw can be up to 20 cm (8 in) across, with sharp, curved claws that can extend and retract.

Actual Size

All the species of tiger live in Asia. Some live in hot jungles, while others live in cold, snowy parts of Russia and China.

Tigers are strong, powerful, and athletic hunters. They can leap 10 m (32.8 ft) and run up to 65 km/h (40 mph).

A tiger has whiskers on its face and on its legs. They are thick, sensitive hairs that help the tiger hunt and move around in the dark. Its facial whiskers can be 15 cm (6 in) long.

A big tiger weighs more than a big lion. A large male tiger weighs as much as three or four people.

Those long canine teeth are the longest teeth of all the big cats. They grow to a length of between 6 and 7.6 cm (2.3–3 in). That's long enough to pierce right through an apple!

How Huge Is an Ostrich?

It is ENORMOUS! It is the tallest and heaviest bird in the world. Ostriches can grow over 2 m (6.5 ft) tall—taller than most pro basketball players.

Huge birds lay huge eggs! An ostrich egg is bigger than any other bird's egg. Each one can weigh the same as 24 hen's eggs.

Actual Size

An ostrich's large eyes help it look out for danger on the African grasslands. Its eyeball is the size of a pool ball.

You can see the difference between males and females by their size and their plumage. Males are mostly black, and females are a brownish shade.

An ostrich is the only bird in the world that has only two toes.

An ostrich is the fastest creature on two legs. It can't run as fast as a cheetah, but it can keep going longer. It could run a marathon in around 45 minutes.

	Top speed
Cheetah	113 km/h (70 mph)
Ostrich	69 km/h (43 mph)
Greyhound	69 km/h (43 mph)
Human Olympic sprinter	32 km/h (20 mph)

An ostrich uses its long legs to zoom around, but also to protect itself. It has a powerful kick that is enough to scare away predators, even lions.

How Scary Is a Snake?

Actual Size

All snakes are hunters, but many of them eat small creatures, and aren't a threat to humans at all. However, some snakes, like this king cobra, have a toxic bite that's strong enough to kill an elephant.

A cobra can lift the front part of its body off the floor and flare its hood to look scary. Its fangs are 8–10 mm (nearly 0.5 in) long and hollow to inject venom into its prey.

The king cobra is the longest venomous snake, but the reticulated python (a constricting snake) is even longer. It can be nearly as long as a stretch limousine!

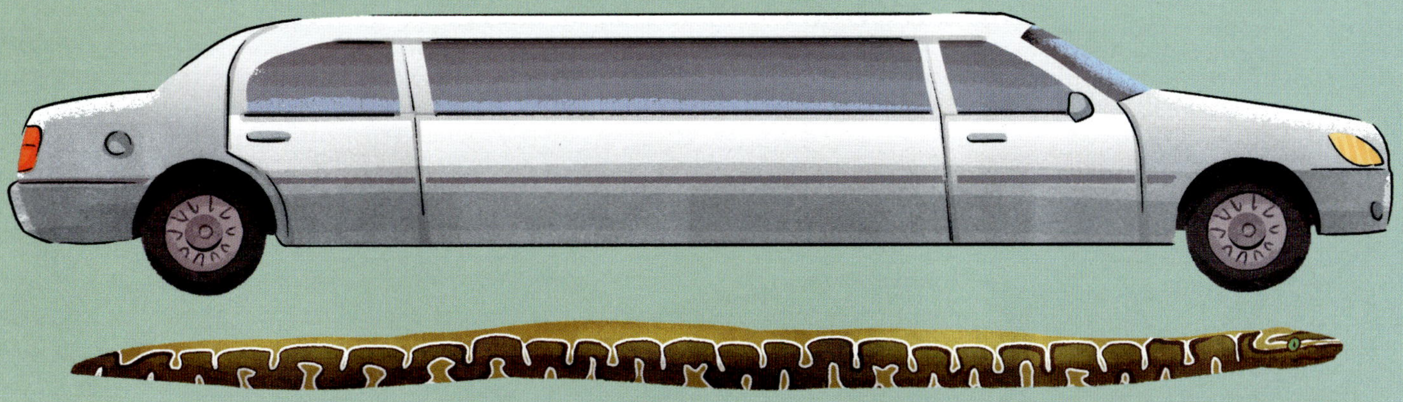

A snake's long, slim body contains a skeleton. Its spine has hundreds of separate bones—anything from 180 to over 400. Most of these have pairs of ribs to protect its organs inside.

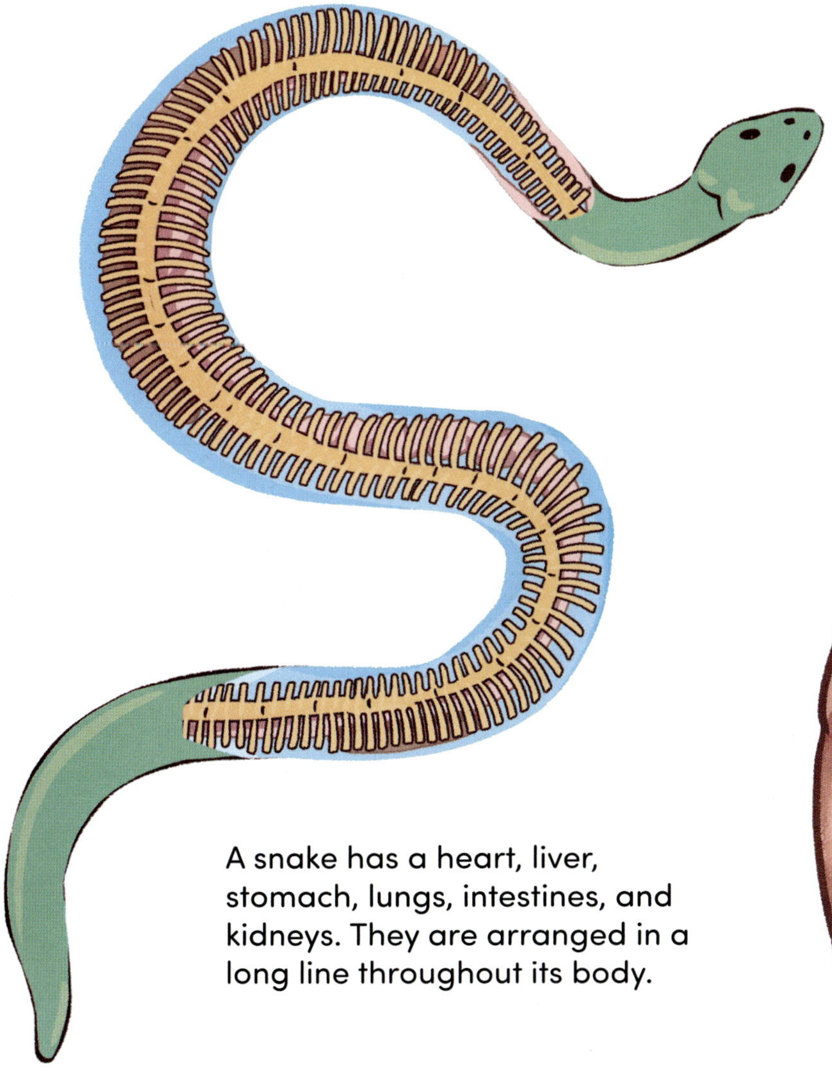

A snake has a heart, liver, stomach, lungs, intestines, and kidneys. They are arranged in a long line throughout its body.

Some snakes—such as blind snakes—are tiny. They live underground and feed on ants, termites, and larvae.

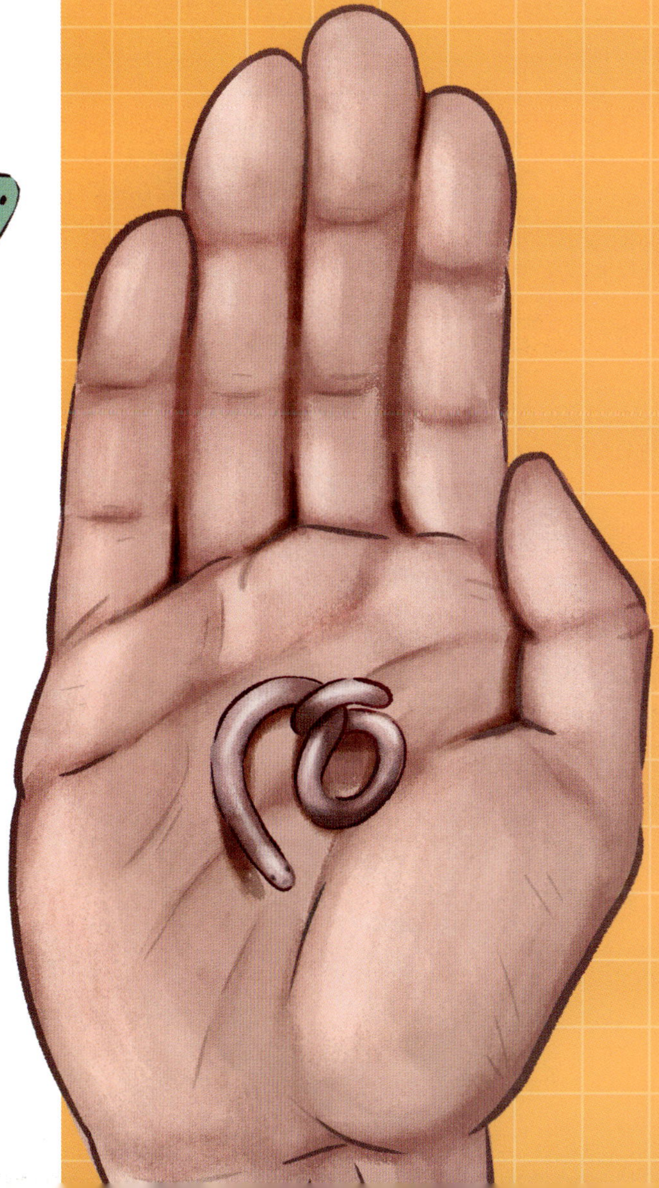

How Small Is a Fennec Fox?

Tiny! It is about the size of a chihuahua dog. The fennec fox is the world's smallest fox, but it is famous for its extremely large ears.

Actual Size

Its ears can grow to be 15 cm (6 in). They help it to listen for prey beneath the ground, and to let body heat escape so it stays cool.

These tiny creatures can jump up to 1 m (3 ft) and run at 32 km/h (20 mph).

The fennec fox lives in the deserts of Africa and burrows underground to stay out of the sun. The foxes are good at digging and their burrows can have tunnels 10 m (33 ft) long.

They come out of their burrow when it is darker and cooler. They use their digging skills to reach prey underground.

Like the red fox, a fennec fox will adapt to eat just about anything it can find. Red foxes are about three or four times bigger than a fennec fox.

How Big Is a Kiwi?

This bird is found only in New Zealand. It is a kiwi, and it is roughly the same size as a domestic chicken. It lives in the forest and cannot fly.

Actual Size

The kiwi is unusual among birds because it uses its sense of smell to find food. It has nostrils on the end of its very long (6 cm/2.4 in) beak.

Using its beak, the kiwi searches for worms. It can smell them 3 cm (over an inch) underground.

The kiwi is quite a small bird but it lays huge eggs for its size. A kiwi's egg is six times bigger than a hen's egg, and up to 25 percent of the kiwi's body size! A human baby is around 5 percent of an adult's body weight.

The yolk of the egg supplies nutrition (food) for the chick inside. One fifth of an ostrich egg is yolk; one third of a hen's egg is yolk; and—you guessed it—a whopping two thirds of a kiwi egg is yolky goodness!

A kiwi doesn't build a nest but instead it digs a burrow in the ground with its sharp claws.

How Enormous Is an Elephant?

An African bush elephant is the biggest creature on land. An adult's trunk is around 2 m (7 ft) long! The trunk is its nose and upper lip combined.

Actual Size

The trunk has over 40,000 muscles inside (but no bones). It is used for breathing, drinking, lifting things, and squirting water.

How do we compare?

	Male human	Male African bush elephant	Male Indian elephant
Height	1.7 m (5.6 ft)	3.3 m (10.8 ft)	3 m (9.8 ft)
Weight	90 kg (200 lb)	6000 kg (13200 lb)	4000 kg (8800 lb)
Ear Size	7 x 4 cm (2.75 x 1.6 in)	1.8 x 1.5 m (6 x 5 ft)	0.9 x 0.6 m (3 x 2 ft)
Top speed*	32 km/h (20 mph)*	40 km/h (25 mph)	25 km/h (16 mph)

*This is the speed of an Olympic sprinter, not an ordinary person!

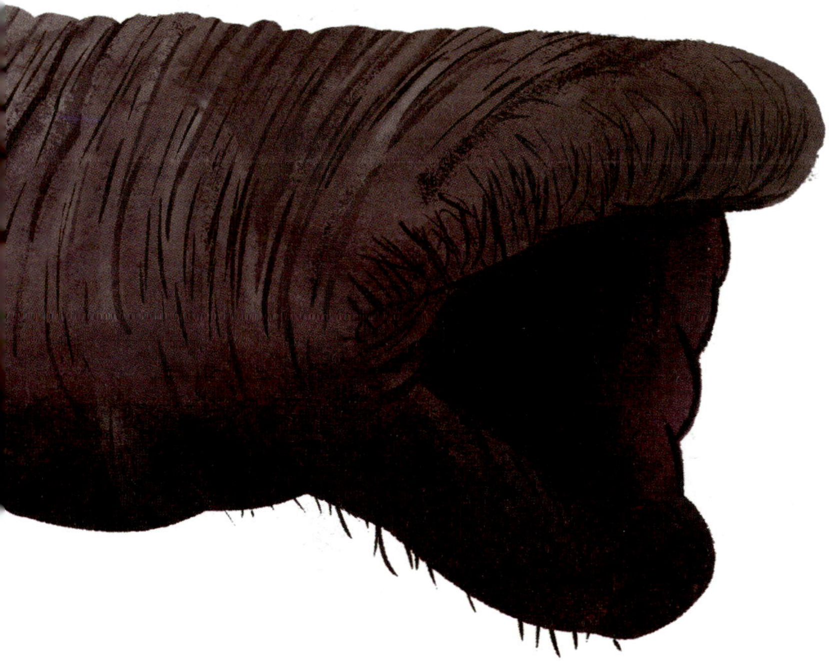

A complete elephant's footprint is as big as a toilet seat! A single toenail is the size of a child's hand.

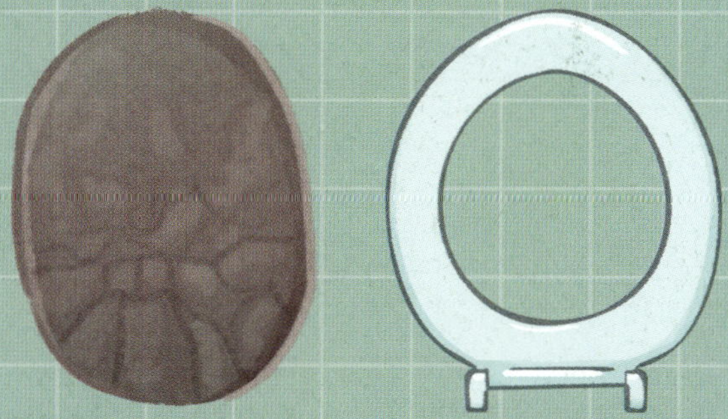

Different species of elephants live in Africa and Asia. Indian elephants live in Asia and have one 'finger' on the end of their trunk. African elephants have two.

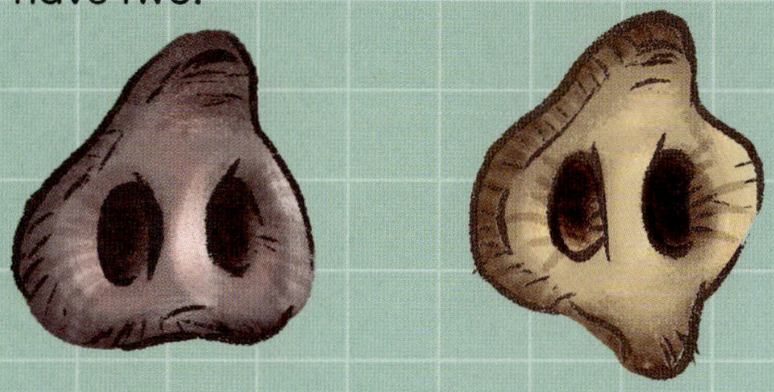

These huge animals walk great distances to find food, and can eat over 130 kg (300 lb) of food every day. They munch on grass, bark, leaves, and roots, using their trunk to rip it up and place it in their mouth.

How Heavy Is a Harpy Eagle?

The harpy eagle lives and hunts in the rain forests of Central and South America. It is one of the world's biggest eagles. The female is bigger than the male, and can weigh up to 9 kg (20lb). That's about the same as two cats.

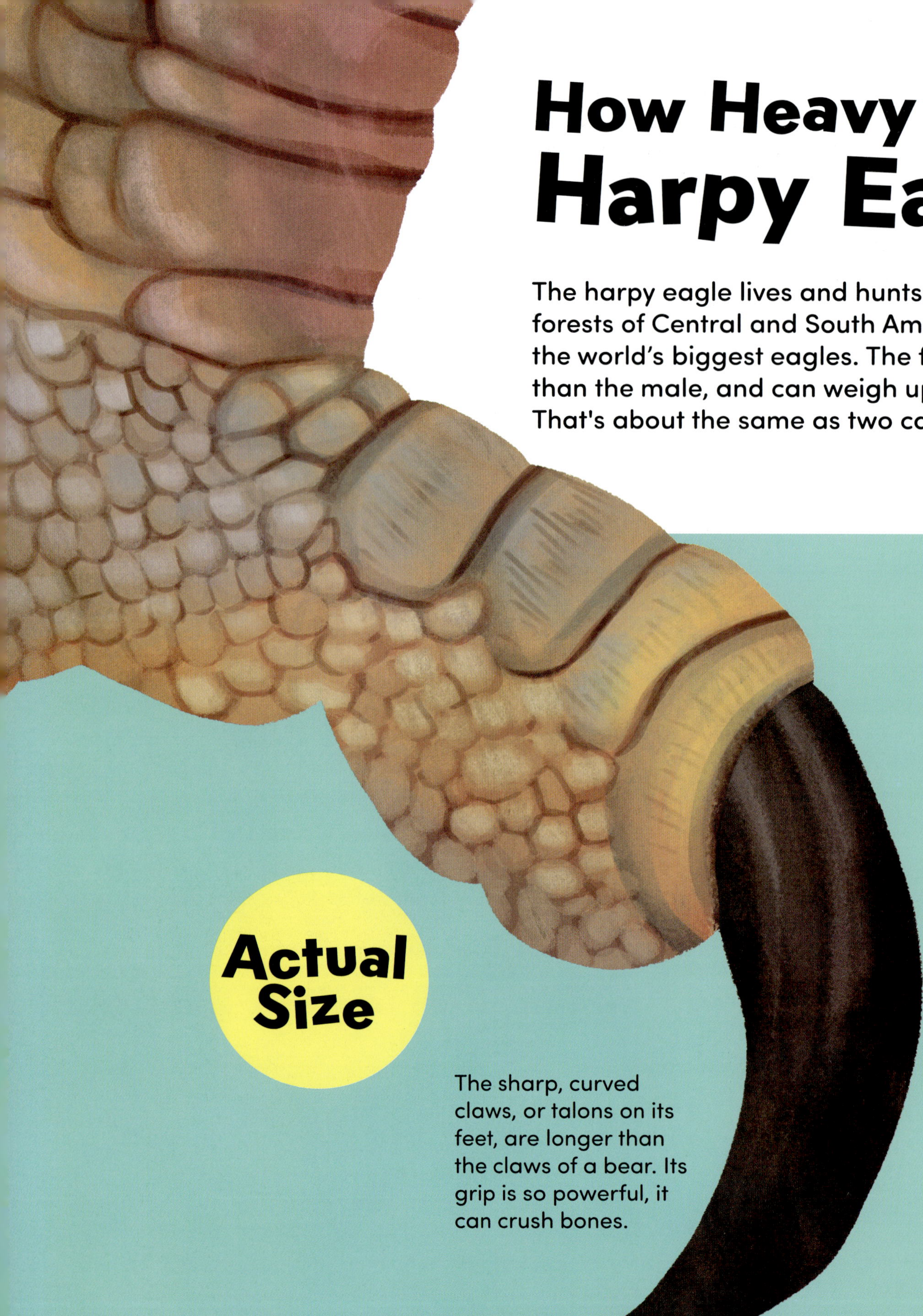

Actual Size

The sharp, curved claws, or talons on its feet, are longer than the claws of a bear. Its grip is so powerful, it can crush bones.

A harpy eagle's wingspan can be up to 2 m (6.5 ft), which is way more than a person with their arms outstretched.

It hunts for medium sized mammals such as sloths and monkeys. A fully-grown female harpy eagle can carry prey that weighs more than a pet cat!

This bird can lift up or lower the feathers around its face. This helps collect sounds so it can hear tiny noises.

It builds a huge nest, balanced high in the fork of a very tall tree. The nest is big enough for you to stretch out across it!

How Big Is a Sun Bear?

The shy sun bear is the smallest type of bear on the planet—but it has an exceptionally long tongue and claws.

Actual Size

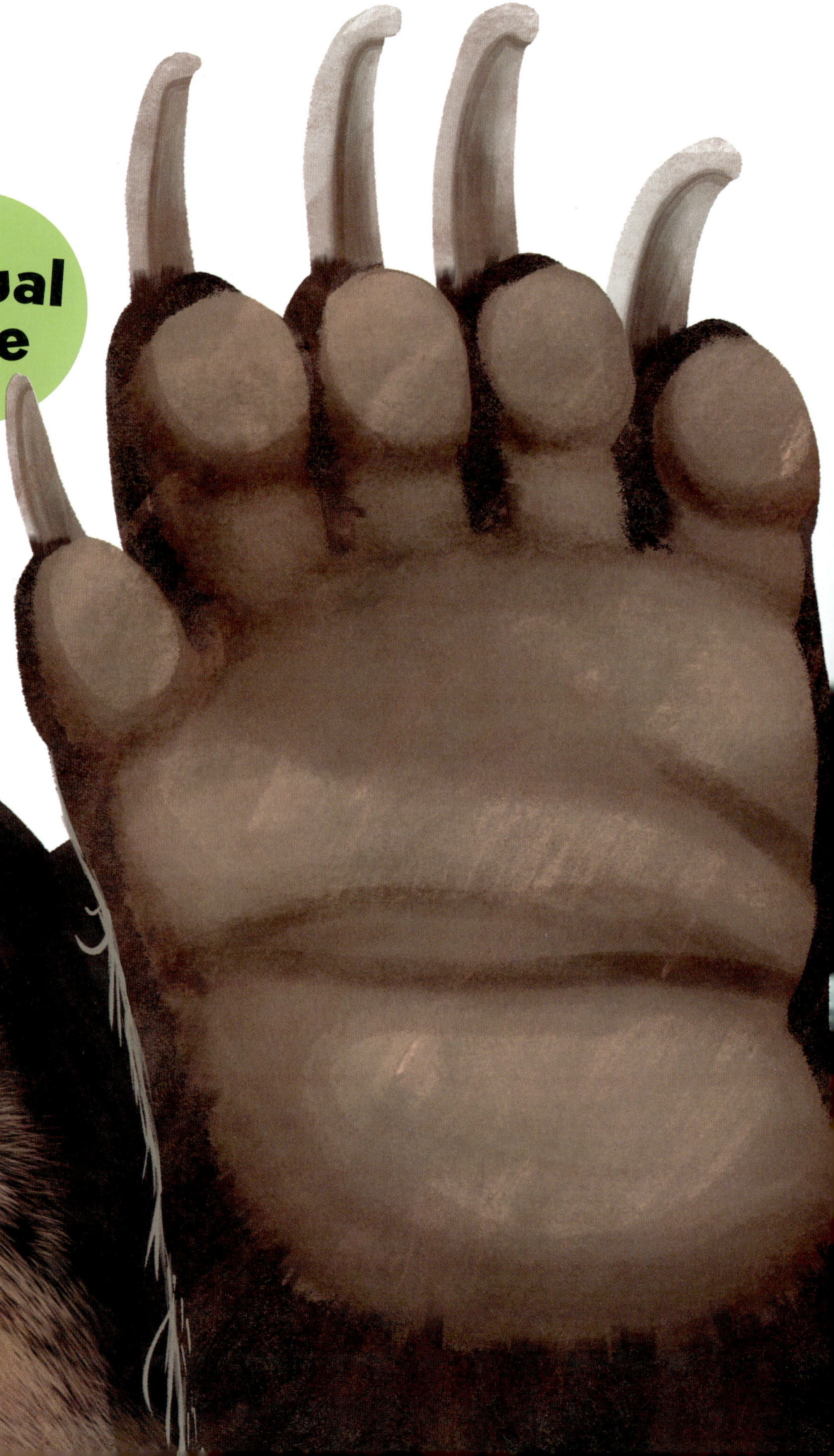

Its claws are strong and curved and used for digging in termite nests, and for climbing trees. Each one can be up to 10 cm (4 in) long.

Its tongue is amazing, growing to 25 cm (10 in) long. It pokes it into insect nests to find honey and grubs.

A sun bear's small size helps it to climb trees more easily.

A fully-grown sun bear only reaches around 1 to 1.5 m (3 to 5 ft) long and less than 1 m (3 ft) tall. That's not much bigger than a German shepherd dog.

How do other bears compare?

polar bear > kodiak bear > panda bear > sun bear

How Big Is a Bat?

There are more than 1,300 species of bat. Some are tiny, some are large. The rare species Kitti's hog-nosed bat is the smallest of them all.

Kitti's hog-nosed bat is possibly the smallest mammal in the world. It isn't much bigger than a bumblebee!

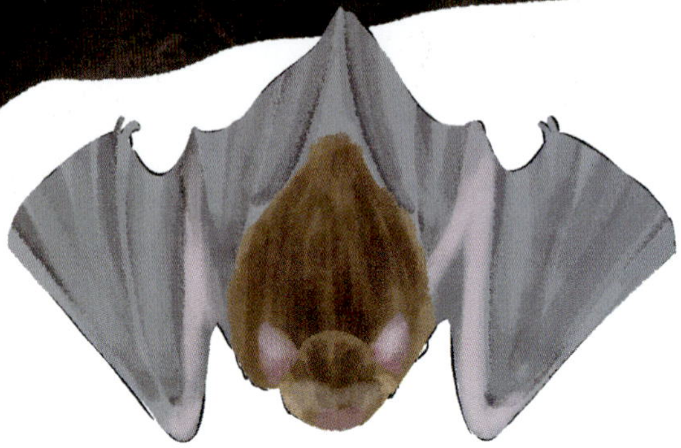

Actual Size

The leaf-nosed bat has a specially shaped nose that is thought to help it hunt for flying insects at night using echolocation.

Lots of bats sleep upside down. They can also eat, poop, and give birth upside down. They hang in trees, or in caves, and simply let go with their feet so they can fly away.

The biggest bats in the world are fruit bats. They are usually active in the daytime. They can weigh as much as a guinea pig!

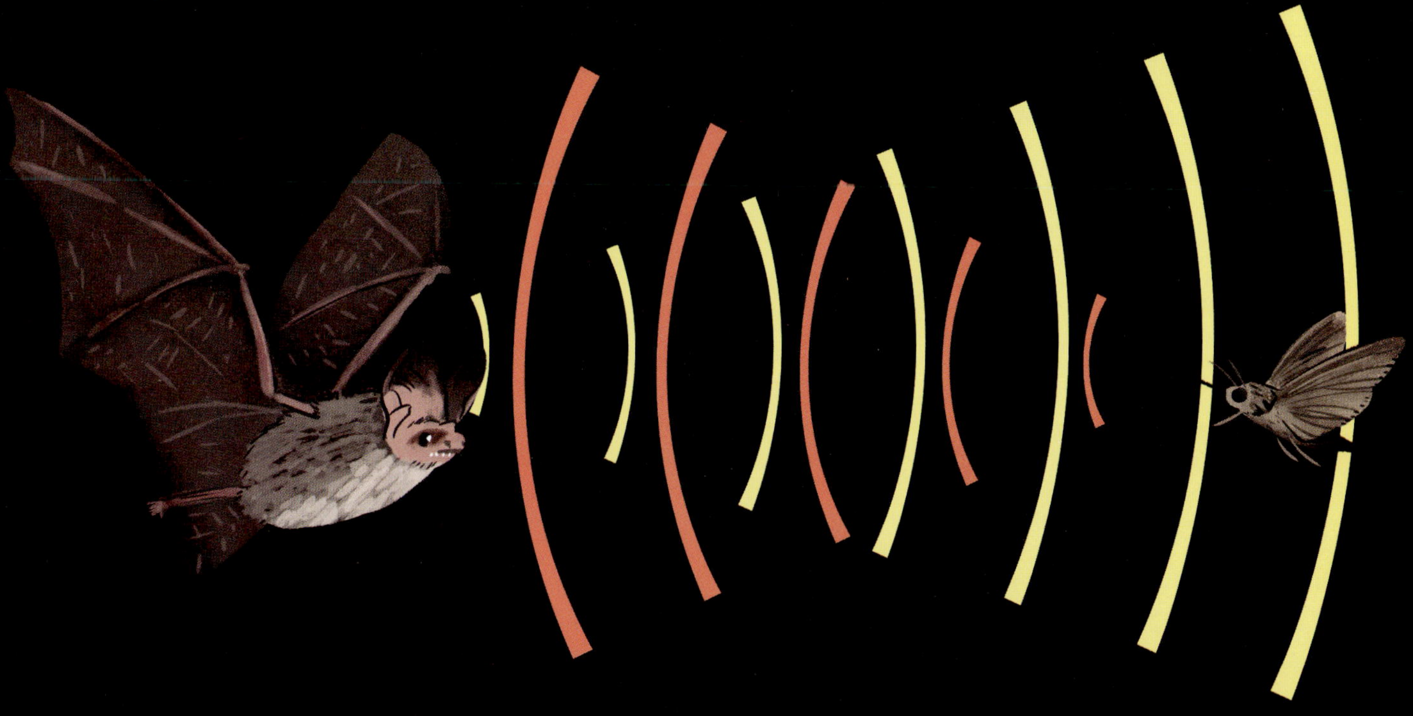

Most bats find their prey, and fly in the darkness, using echolocation. The bat sends out sounds from its mouth or nose, and listens to the echoes to make a map of what is around it.

How Big Is an Aye-Aye?

The aye-aye is an odd-looking type of nocturnal lemur from Madagascar. It is around 40 cm (16 in) long (slightly smaller than a red squirrel), with an even longer tail.

Actual Size

This is an aye-aye compared to a toddler.

Its large ears help it to hear wood-boring insects under the bark of a tree. It also has big eyes, to help it see more in the darkness.

Its tail can be up to 60 cm (24 in) long. That's over twice the length of this page!

As well as eating grubs, it also feeds on fruit, seeds, and nectar. Its front teeth poke forward and never stop growing.

Its thinnest finger has a special joint that allows it to rotate (move around) a full 360 degrees.

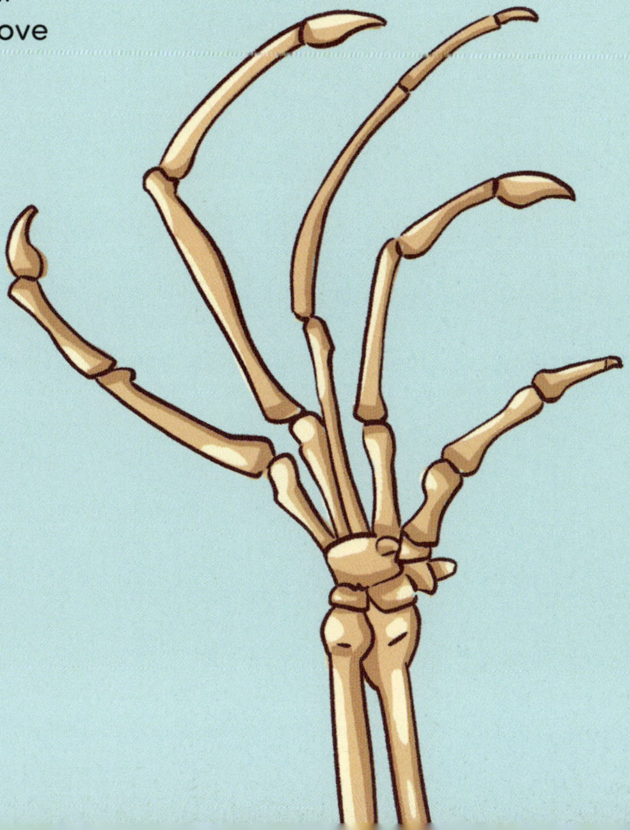

Its third finger is long, thin, and bony, and grows up to 8 cm (3 in) long. The aye-aye uses it to tap on trees to find grubs under the bark. Then it makes a hole and pokes its fourth, even longer finger inside to pull out the grubs.

How Big Is an Ant?

There are thousands and thousands of species of ant on the planet. Some are less than 1 mm (0.04 in) big—the size of this full stop. Others grow to 5 cm (2 in) long. These leafcutter ants are 1 cm (1.3 in long).

Actual Size

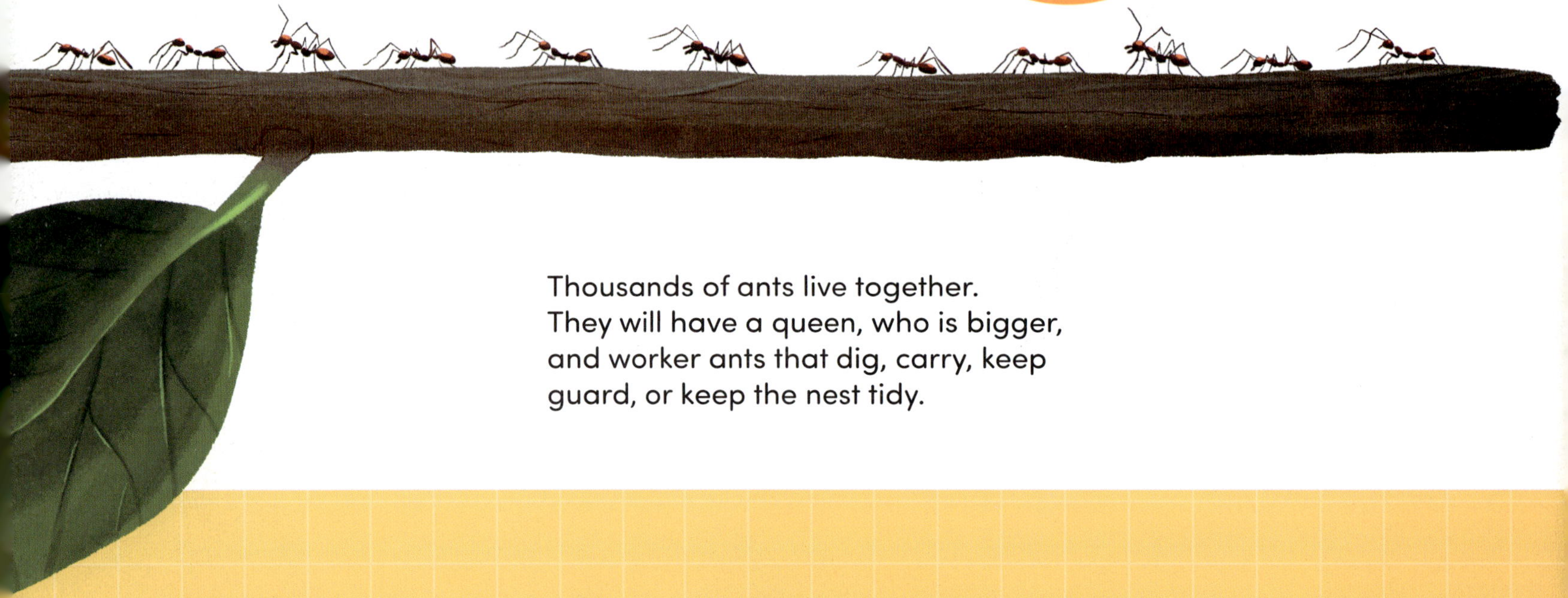

Thousands of ants live together. They will have a queen, who is bigger, and worker ants that dig, carry, keep guard, or keep the nest tidy.

Leafcutter ants use their mouthparts (called mandibles) to cut pieces of leaf. They don't eat the leaves, but carry them to their nest to bury underground.

Fungus grows on the leaves, which is what the ants eat.

Leafcutter ants are medium-sized ants, but they are famous for their strength. They can carry pieces of plant 50 times their body weight across the rain forest floor.

How Huge Is a Humpback Whale?

Pretty huge! They weigh around 36,000 kg (40 tons) and are too heavy to survive on land. Their weight is more than 35 Formula 1 cars—including their drivers!

Whales don't rely on their eyesight under water, and their eyes are relatively small. A humpback's eyesight is about ten times worse than a person's.

Actual Size

A humpback's tail flukes are around 5.5 m (18 ft) wide—the length of two kayaks.

A humpback whale is longer than a school bus and its mouth is up to 3 m (10 ft) wide. Its fins are longer than those of many whales—they are one third of its body length.

How Big Is a Beaver?

A beaver is a type of rodent, like a rat. Beavers are the second largest rodents on the planet after capybaras (which live in South America).

Actual Size

Different types of beaver live in Europe and North America. The North American beaver grows to 1.3 m (4.3 ft) long including its tail—longer than a golf club).

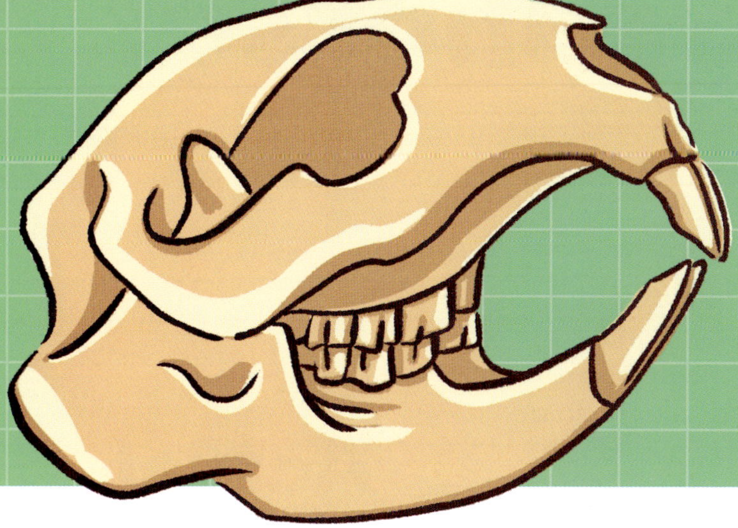

Beavers are well known for their teeth. They never stop growing, so although gnawing through wood grinds their teeth down, they soon grow long again.

A beaver's flat, paddle-shaped tail is up to 0.30 m (1 ft) long. It helps the beaver steer when swimming, or sit upright on land.

Its back feet are big and webbed to help it swim.

A beaver gnaws through trees to build a dam. This creates a pond for the beaver to build its home, called a lodge. The lodge can be higher than your ceiling and as big as three large beds side-by-side.

How Small Is a Seahorse?

Seahorses come in a variety of sizes.
The smallest is the pygmy seahorse which lives on coral reefs in Southeast Asia.

The tiny adult pygmy seahorses (shown here) have even tinier babies. They are smaller than a grain of rice!

Actual Size

Many species, like this yellow seahorse, suck up tiny shrimps with their snout. Some can eat up to 3,000 brine shrimp in a day!

The dorsal (back) fin moves rapidly to push the seahorse through the water. Most seahorses can only swim very slowly, but they can move forward, backward, and up and down.

A seahorse has a prehensile tail that allows it to hold on tightly to seaweed or coral so it can rest.

A standard seahorse is about the height of an apple.

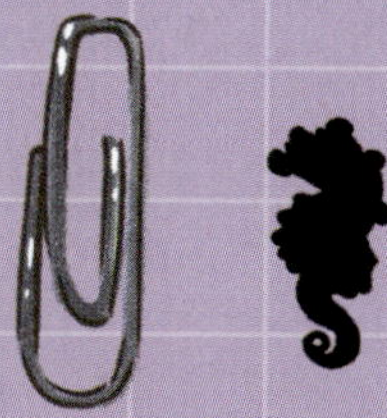

A pygmy seahorse is smaller than a paper clip.

The big-belly seahorse is the biggest in the world. It can grow up to 30 cm (1 ft) long—longer than an electric toothbrush.

How Cool Is a Koala?

Very cool—its body temperature is lower than most other mammals. They chill out in other ways, too, by sleeping for up to 19 hours a day.

A koala has three fingers and two thumbs!

Actual Size

A koala's claws are strong and curved to help with its life in the trees. Each one can be 2.5 cm (1 in) long.

When a koala isn't sleeping, it is usually eating! Koalas feed at night and can munch between 0.5 and 1 kg (1 to 2 lb) of eucalyptus leaves. That's a lot of leaves, but not much nutrition.

A koala's brain is small for its overall size. Brains use a lot of energy, and the koala's diet doesn't give it enough nutrients to support a big brain.

A koala is a marsupial, so its newborn baby crawls into a pouch on its mother's belly to stay safe while it grows. A newborn is only the size of a jelly bean! When it is big enough, it will ride on its mother's back.

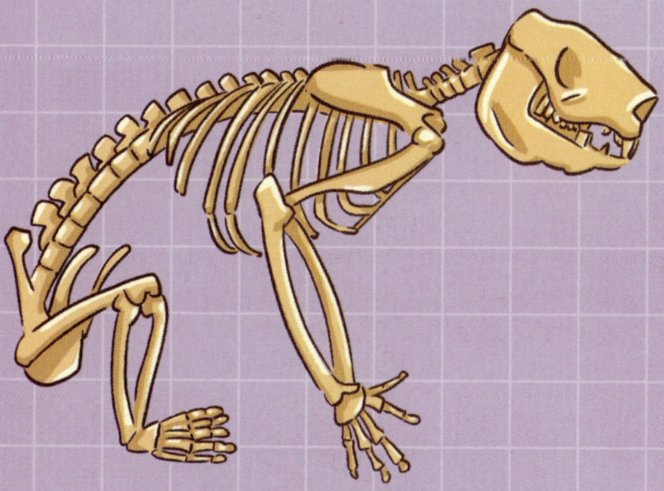

Many mammals have 13 pairs of ribs, but a koala has only 11 pairs.

A tarantula rubs its legs together to flick hairs from its body at any creature that comes too close. These tiny hairs get caught in the eyes of predators to put them off.

How Big Is a Tarantula?

Tarantulas vary in size, but they can get pretty huge. The one shown on this page is a Goliath bird-eating spider—the biggest spider on the planet! When its legs are spread out, it's nearly the size of a dinner plate.

This spider is a predator, feeding on frogs, small rodents, and insects. It has huge fangs for injecting venom. They are hollow and 2.5 cm (1 in) long.

A tarantula's bite would hurt you, but not kill you. Some spiders, however, have strong enough venom to kill a person. Australia's funnel web spiders, for example, are only 5 cm (2 in) long but can be lethal.

A tarantula is about the same size as a teacup.

Tarantulas are not the only large spiders. The giant huntsman spider has legs that would cover a dinner plate, but its body is smaller and lighter than that of a tarantula.

These giant huntsman spiders can run quickly, covering nearly 1 m (over 3 ft) in a second!

How Big Is a Walrus?

A walrus is an ocean creature that can reach huge sizes. It can be 3 m (nearly 10 ft) long and weigh as much as a small car!

Actual Size

A walrus has between 400 and 700 whiskers on its snout. Some measure up to 30 cm (1 ft) long. They help the walrus find food on the ocean floor.

Its tusks are overgrown teeth. They can be nearly 1 m (about 3 ft) long—around the length of a tennis racquet.

These animals live in the icy Arctic, so they have thick, bumpy skin with a layer of blubber (fat) underneath. The blubber can be 15 cm (6 in) thick to keep them warm.

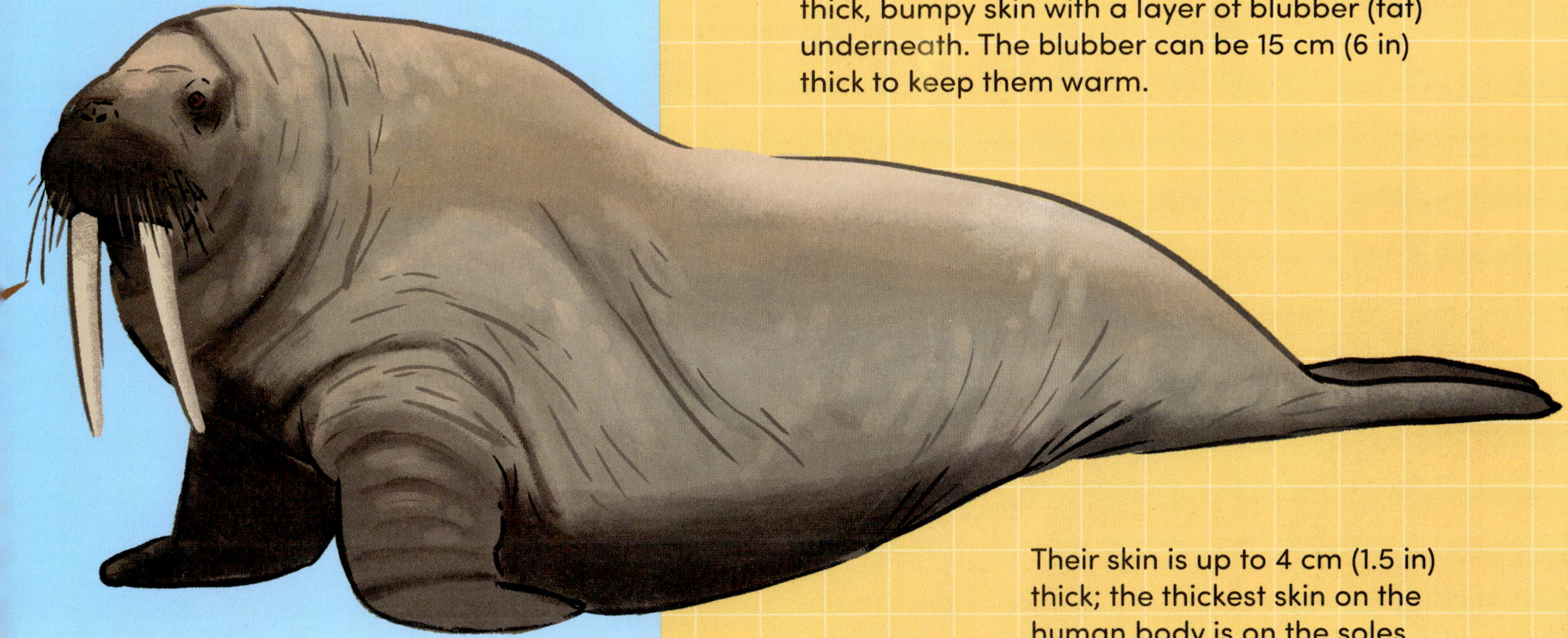

Their skin is up to 4 cm (1.5 in) thick; the thickest skin on the human body is on the soles of the feet and is only 0.4 cm (0.15 in) thick!

A baby walrus is called a calf. A newborn calf weighs 45–75 kg (100–165 lb), compared to a human baby that weighs 2.7–3.6 kg (6–8 lb). That's up to 20 times heavier!

How Long Is an Anteater's Tongue?

Actual Size

It's almost too long to fit on this page! It can reach 60 cm (24 in) in length and is used for lapping up bugs to eat.

The giant anteater has no teeth. It doesn't need to chew its food, as it eats ants, termites, and other insects, licking up around 30,000 each day.

Females give birth to one baby at a time. They are called pups.

They ride on their mother's back when they are little.

From the tip of its nose to the end of its bushy tail, a giant anteater measures between 1.8 and 2.4 m (6 to 8 ft). Its tail is nearly half of that length.

Its skinny tongue is covered in spikes and sticky saliva to help it gather insects. It can flick its tongue in and out up to 150 times in a minute!

How do we compare?

	Female human	Female anteater
Height	1.6 m (5.25 ft)	2.15 m (7 ft)
Weight	65 kg (144 lb)	45 kg (100 lb)
Tail length	none!	0.9 m (3 ft)
Pregnancy	40 weeks	27 weeks

How Big is a Tortoise?

Tortoises vary in size. Some species are small and some are HUGE! The one shown here is a speckled tortoise, the smallest type of tortoise in the world.

Actual Size

A baby speckled tortoise is only 3 cm (1.2 in) long—the size of a walnut—and weighs less than a silver coin.

The giant tortoise grows to around 1.35 m (4.5 ft) in length and weighs 300–400 kg (650–900 lb). That's at least the weight of four people!

The top of a tortoise's shell is domed and patterned. It is called the carapace. The spine attaches to this piece.

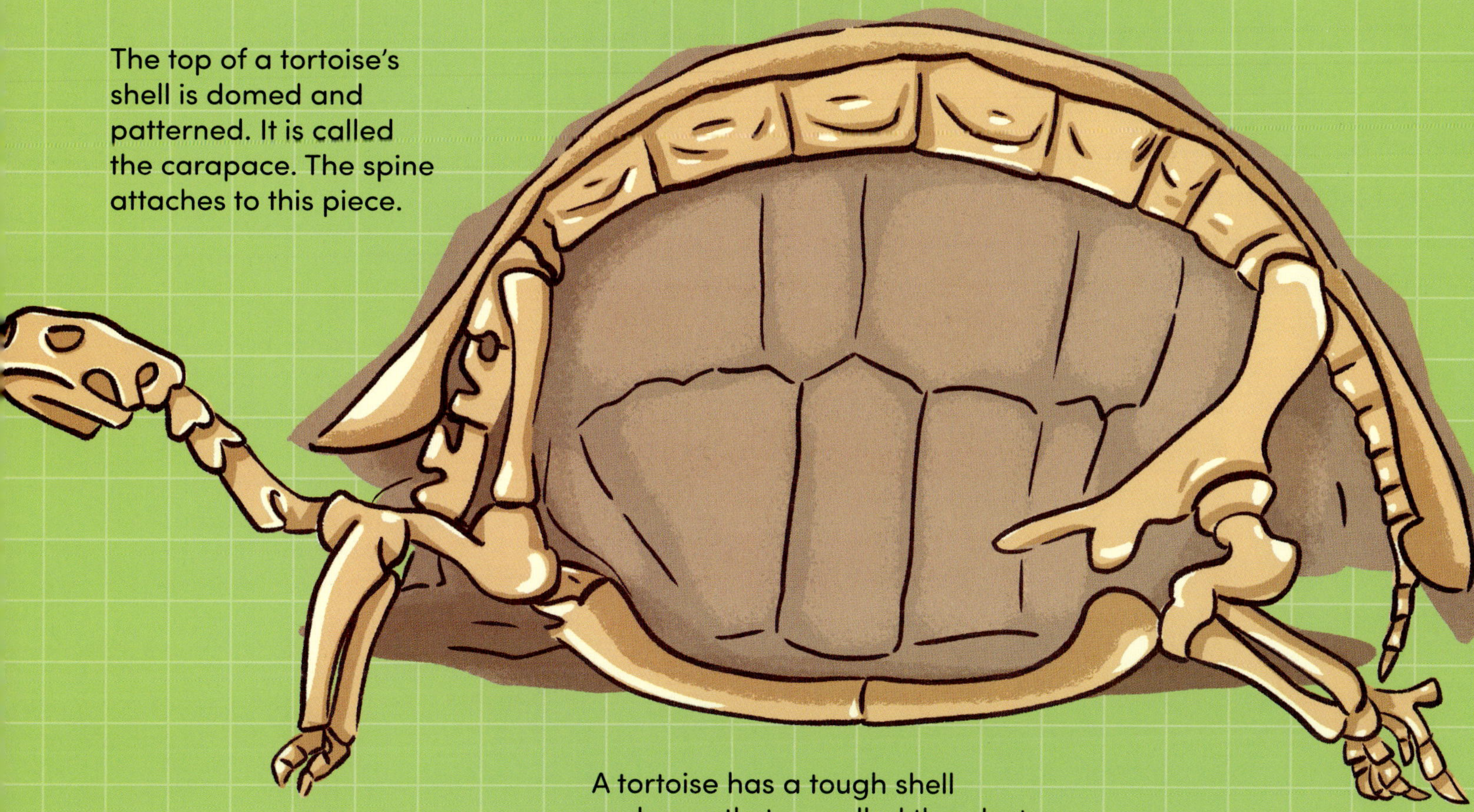

A tortoise has a tough shell underneath, too, called the plastron. It is connected to the carapace.

Tortoises are reptiles, so they lay eggs. The baby will hatch as a male or a female depending on the temperature when it is inside the egg.

How Big Is a Frog?

Red frogs are small but deadly. Their skin contains a toxin that can cause numbness, paralysis, or even death for their predators.

They are found in the rain forests of Central America. Not all of them are red: there are blue, yellow, green, and black ones, and a host of shades in between.

The golden poison frog is slightly bigger, and it is the most toxic frog on the planet. It has enough toxin to kill 10 grown men.

In contrast, the Goliath frog is a HUGE beast! The biggest frog in the world, it can be 30 cm (1 ft) long and weigh as much as a pet cat!

Most types of frog eat insects and worms. Their eyes move down into their head as they swallow, to push food down their throat.

Several types of frog, like this Wallace's flying frog, have such big feet that they can glide through the air! They live in the trees and can launch themselves from the branches.

How Big Is a Cuttlefish?

There are over 120 species of cuttlefish. Many are as long as your hand, but some grow twice that size or more.

These eight-legged ocean creatures are related to squids and octopuses. As well as their eight arms, cuttlefish have two long tentacles on their head. These are stored in a pouch when they are not being used to capture prey.

Actual Size

Its long tentacles are used to grab prey and also for tasting. They have suckers on the ends.

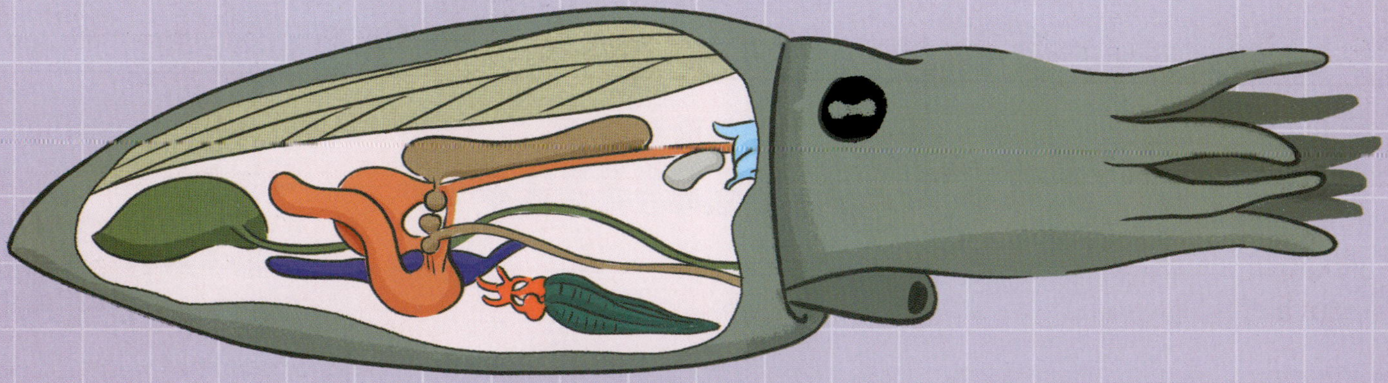

Cuttlefish have three hearts and green blood! One heart pumps blood around its body, and the other two pump blood over its gills for breathing.

A cuttlefish can take in water and then squirt it out to push itself backward.

These creatures are camouflage champions. They have 10 million cells in their skin to change their pattern, shade, and even texture.

How Giant Is a Giant Armadillo?

This South American mammal can grow over 1 m (3.25 ft) and that's not including its 50 cm (20 in) tail!

Its ENORMOUS middle claws are used to dig, to make a burrow, or to rip apart a termite mound. For its body size, they are the biggest claws of any animal on Earth.

How do we compare?

	10-year-old human	Adult female armadillo
Height	1.37 m (4.5 ft)	0.3–0.6 m (1–2 ft)
Weight	32 kg (70 lb)	20–32 kg (44–70 lb)
Tail length	none!	0.5 m (1.6 ft)
Top speed	14 km/h (9 mph)	48 km/h (30 mph)

Armadillos are covered in bands, or stripes, of scales. They are tough like fingernails, with softer skin in between so the animals can bend.

The giant armadillo has more teeth than any other mammal—up to 100!

Armadillos are more agile than they look, and can trot through the forest quickly. They can also stand up, using their strong tail to help them balance.

How Small Is a Chameleon?

Some are tiny! The nano-chameleon is found on the island of Madagascar and is only about the size of a sunflower seed.

Many chameleons, though, are bigger than this. There are over 200 species, and the largest grow to 0.6 m (2 ft) long.

The male Jackson's chameleon has three horns and grows to around 30 cm (1 ft) long.

Chameleons are well adapted to climbing trees. They have two toes that point in one direction and three that point in the other. This helps them to grip onto branches.

A chameleon's eyes are amazing. Each one can move separately and see different things, allowing it a view of everything around it.

Chameleons are famous for their changing coloration. This panther chameleon is showing off to try to attract a mate.

Many chameleons have a tongue that is nearly twice their body length. If humans were the same, your tongue could be around 2.5 m (8 ft) long!

How Scary Is a **Shark?**

Some sharks are enormous with a mouthful of razor sharp teeth. This dwarf lantern shark, however, is tiny and harmless. It is the world's smallest shark.

Actual Size

It feeds on krill, which are tiny shrimp-like creatures, and lives in deep water. Its skin has organs that give off light, so it can glow like a lantern or fade into the shadows.

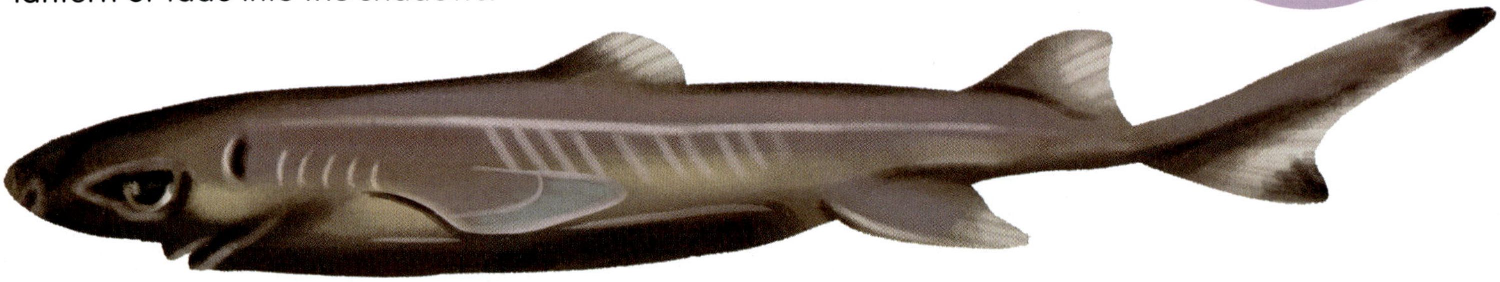

Some sharks, including reef sharks, have a pale underside and darker back. This is a type of camouflage known as countershading.

From below, the pale belly makes the shark hard to see against the light shining through the water. From above, the dark top side hides the shark against the darker waters underneath.

The world's biggest shark is the whale shark. Its mouth is around 1.4 m (4.5 ft) wide, but it only eats plankton and small fish.

How Strong Is a Mantis Shrimp?

This small but spectacular shrimp really punches above its weight! It uses its two claws like hammers to stun prey or defend itself against attackers.

Actual Size

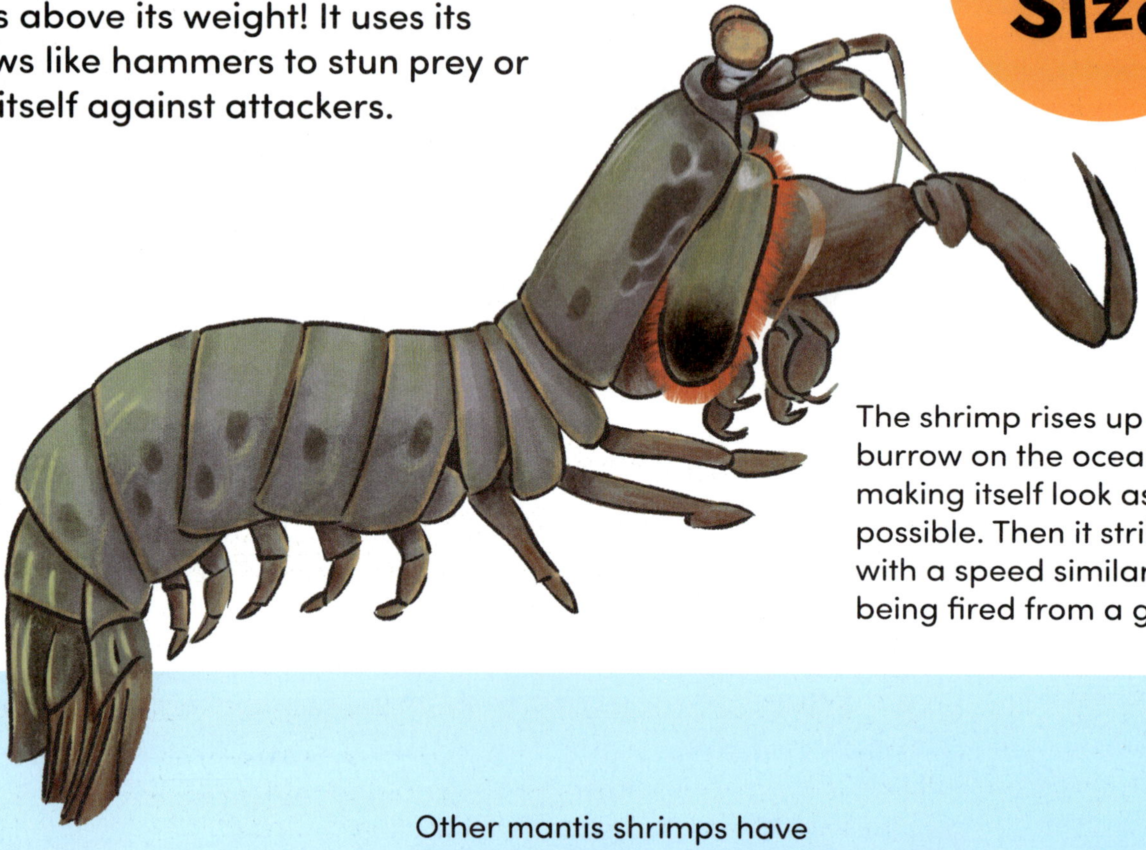

The shrimp rises up from its burrow on the ocean floor, making itself look as large as possible. Then it strikes—BAM!—with a speed similar to a bullet being fired from a gun.

Other mantis shrimps have spear-like limbs and stab their predators.

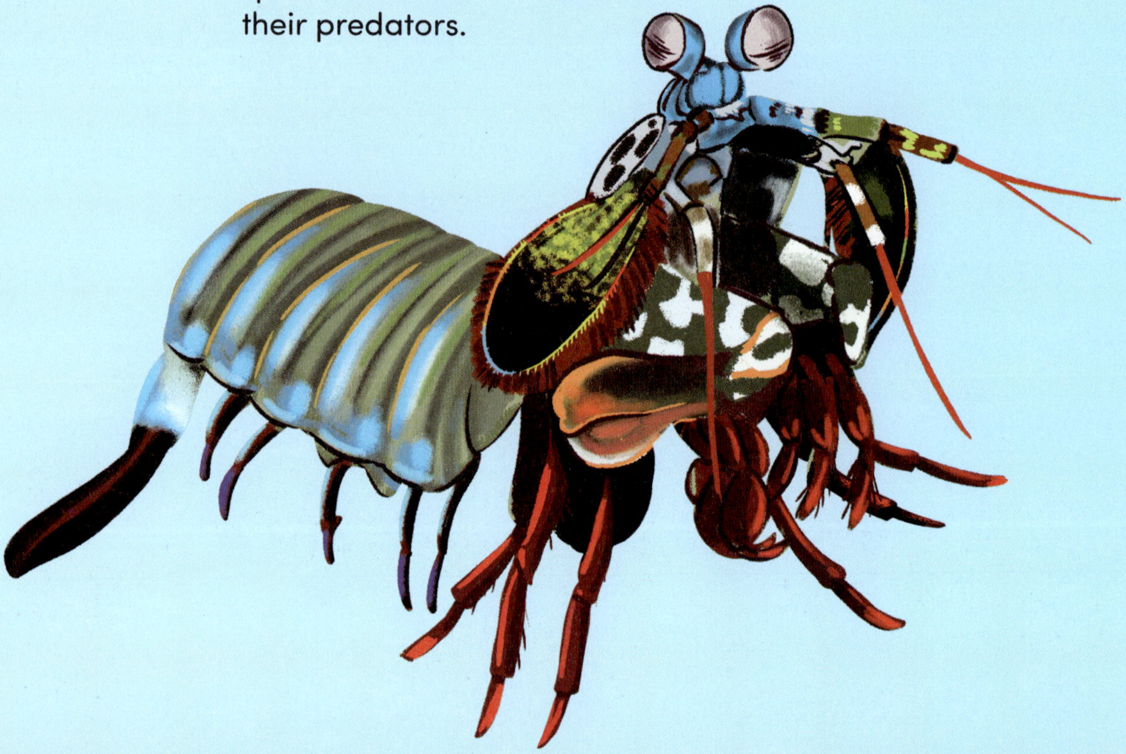

These mantis shrimps can see all you can, and they can see in infrared and ultraviolet, too.

They have the most complex eyes ever seen in nature. Each eye has up to 16 types of cone cell, which sense different wavelengths of light. A human eye has only three!

Mantis shrimps are related to lobsters. They have three pairs of legs in the middle of their body for walking. Behind that, they have smaller legs that help them to swim.

The body of these shrimps is protected by a hard shell called a carapace.

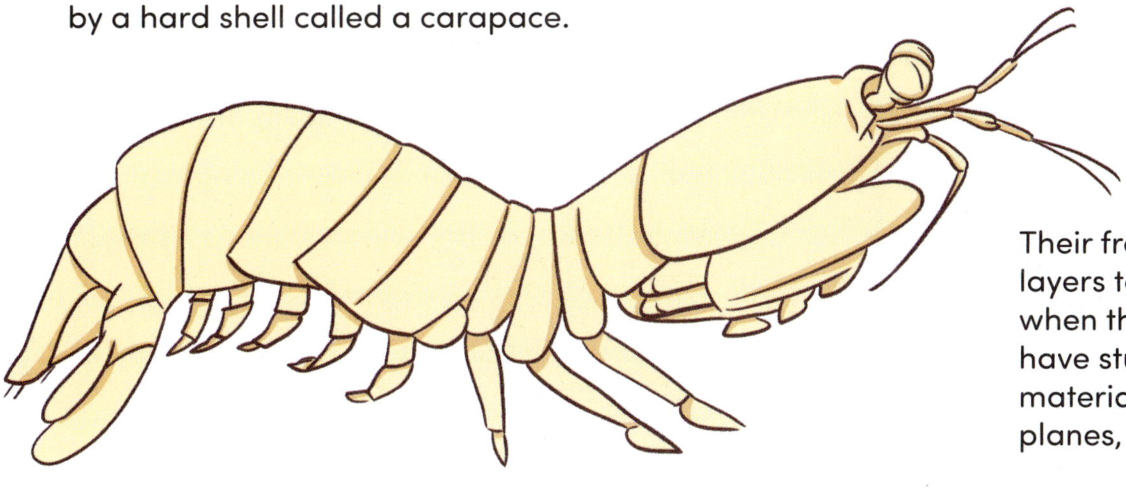

Their front limbs have extra layers to protect them when they punch. Scientists have studied their cells for materials to make cars, planes, and army clothing.

How Big Is a Termite?

Termites are social insects and live in large colonies. Each termite is adapted to a different role within the nest. Life in a colony revolves around a queen, who can be up to 15 cm (6 in) long.

Most of the termites will be workers, which are much smaller than their queen. Bigger termites called soldiers protect the nest.

Actual Size

Workers have several jobs. They feed the queen, build the nest, keep things clean, and look after eggs.

When they are ready to reproduce, some termites grow wings. These termites are called alates. They swarm in the air looking for a mate. After a male and female alate form a pair, they land and break off their wings. At this point they become dealates.

The delate pair make a new nest and the female lays eggs. The new king and queen look after the first generation of their offspring until there are enough workers and soldiers in the colony to do the job.

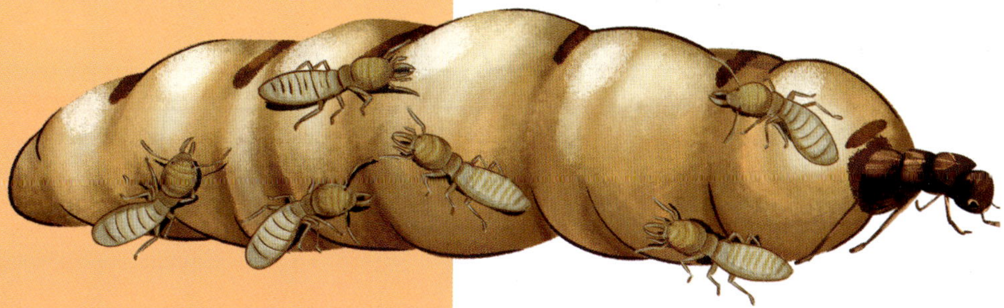

As she lays more eggs, the queen grows bigger and bigger. She can live for at least 10 years and produce millions of eggs.

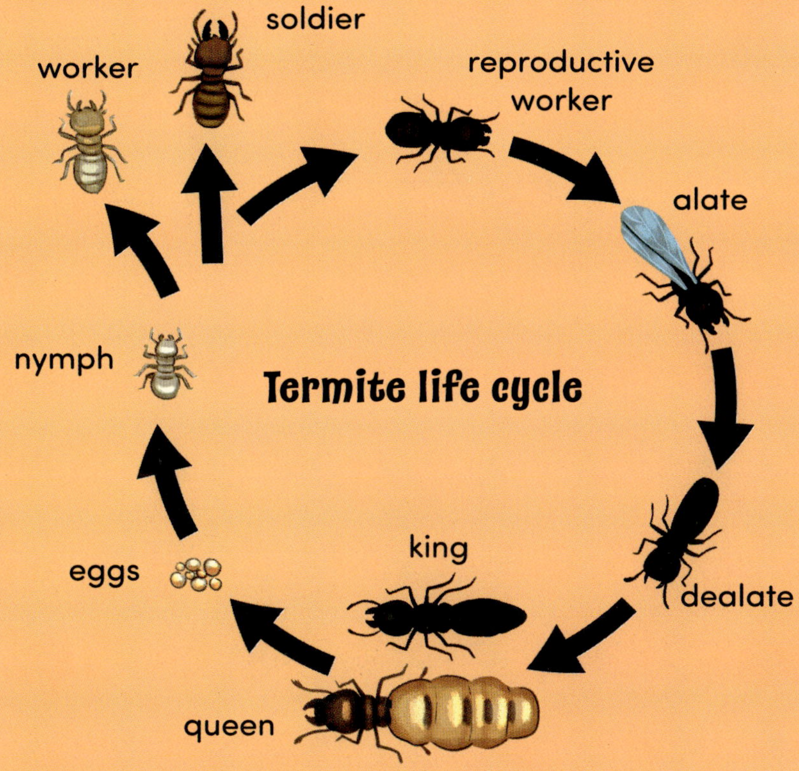

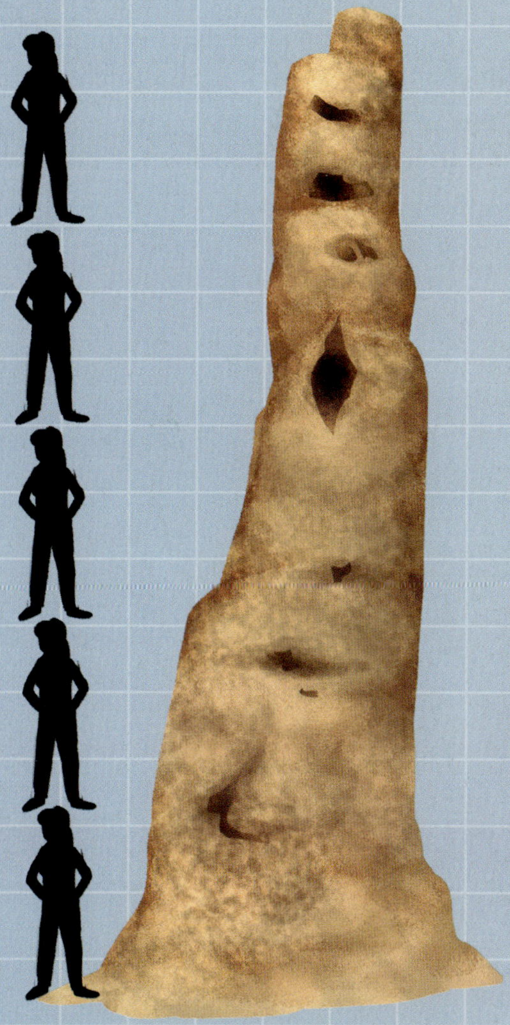

Some termites live underground, but others build huge mounds from soil and saliva that can be as tall as five people.

How do we compare?

	Human	Termites
Classification	Mammal Primate	Insect Isoptera
Legs	2	6
Evolved	More than 315,000 years ago	More than 251,000,000 years ago
Reproduction	Babies	Eggs
Life span	70–90 years	10–25 years (queen)

How Big Is a Star-Nosed Mole?

This crazy creature is about the size of a rat, and is an animal kingdom record breaker! It is one of the fastest diggers of all animals and can swim and dive well, too.

Actual Size

Its nose has 22 tentacles, helping it to track down prey and sense its surroundings. It can even smell underwater, which is a rare talent.

It has strong, sharp claws for digging tunnels. It lives in the dark and is virtually blind.

The star-shaped nose is exceptionally sensitive. It contains over 100,000 nerve endings. That's over five times more than your hand, all in a space the size of a fingertip.

It is one of the fastest eaters on the planet! It takes only a quarter of a second to identify, grab, and gobble down its prey—usually a worm or a grub.

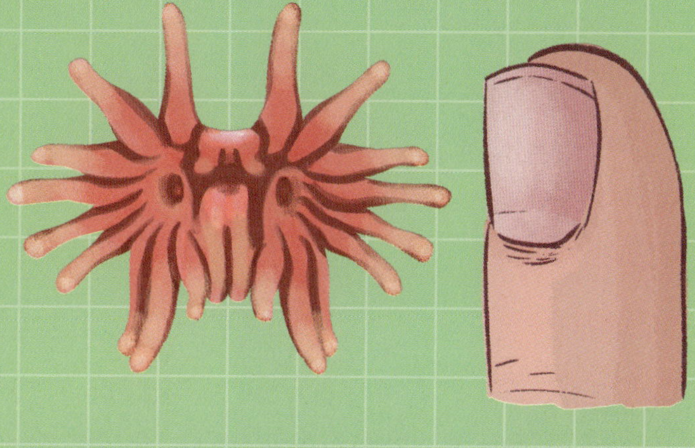

How Dangerous Is a Komodo Dragon?

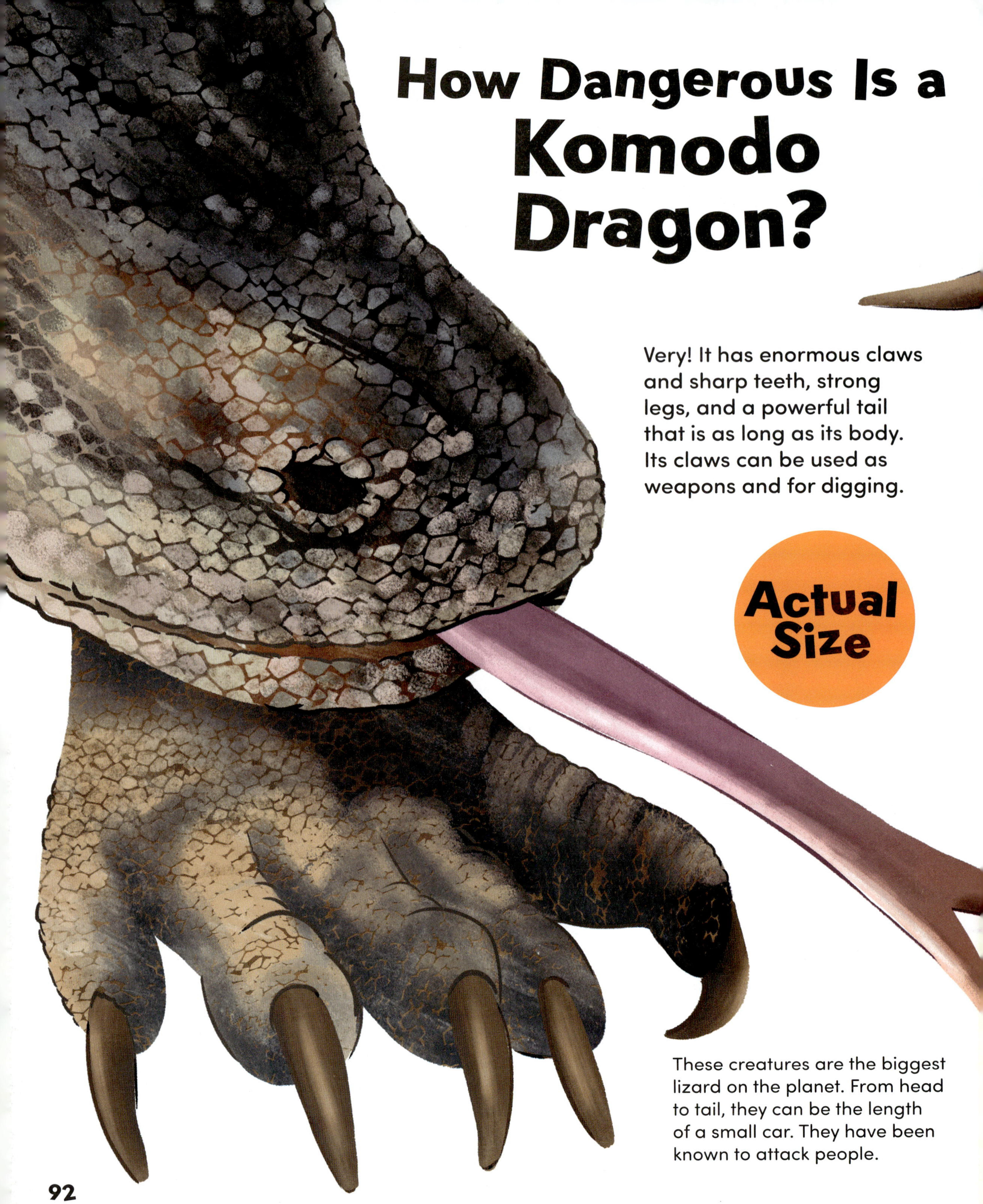

Very! It has enormous claws and sharp teeth, strong legs, and a powerful tail that is as long as its body. Its claws can be used as weapons and for digging.

These creatures are the biggest lizard on the planet. From head to tail, they can be the length of a small car. They have been known to attack people.

They're pretty quick and can reach speeds of 20 km/h (12 mph) for short sprints—much faster than a person.

A Komodo dragon flicks its forked tongue in and out to pick up smells in the air. It can "taste" these scents from several miles away.

Its stomach expands so it can eat up to 80 percent of its own weight in one meal.

Their mouth is full of nasty, bacteria-filled saliva that can kill a large animal if bitten. They may also have a venom gland inside their mouth.

A Komodo dragon can grow to a length of 3 m (9.8 feet).

Invertebrates

Invertebrates are divided into many different groups including insects, arachnids, jellyfish, mollusks, squid, and gastropods. Many of them have a hard outer shell called an exoskeleton. Examples in this book: rhinoceros beetle, butterfly, snail, hornet, ant, tarantula, cuttlefish.

Vertebrates

These are divided into the following groups.

Mammal

These warm-blooded creatures give birth to live young and feed them with their mother's milk. They mostly have fur or hair on their body. Examples in this book: gorilla, jerboa, lion, sloth, koala, orca, bat, beaver, anteater, whale.

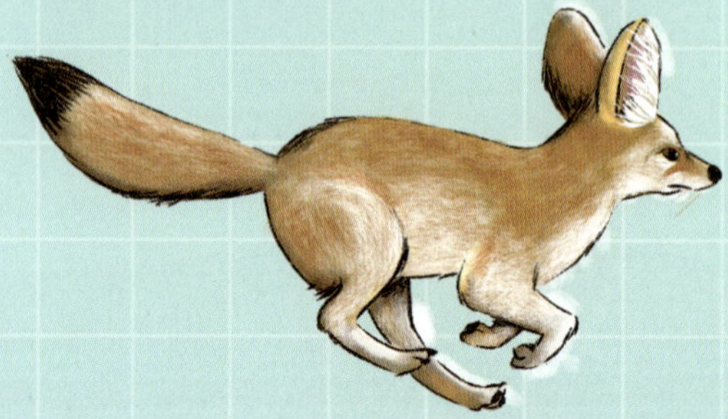

Bird

These creatures have wings, feathers, and a beak or bill. They lay eggs and many of them can fly. Examples in this book: hummingbird, toucan, ostrich, kiwi, eagle.

Glossary

Baleen Bony strips in the jaw of whales that feed by filtering food from the ocean.

Canine tooth A sharp front tooth used for tearing meat.

Colony A group of insects that are all related and work together to survive.

Constrictor A snake that kills its prey by winding around it and squeezing until its prey can't breathe.

Diurnal Active during the daytime (compare to nocturnal.)

Domestic Living with people, instead of in the wild.

Dorsal fin A fin on the back of a sea creature such as a fish or a whale.

Eucalyptus An evergreen tree found in Australia with strong smelling leaves.

Grub The larva of some insects; they look like short, fat worms.

Incisor tooth The very front teeth with flat edges for cutting food.

Invertebrate A creature without a spine, including insects, spiders, worms, crabs, and squid.

Keratin A hard substance which makes nails, horns, beaks, and feathers.

Larva (plural: larvae) An insect after it hatches from an egg, but before it becomes an adult.

Mandibles The lower jaw bone of a mammal or biting mouthparts of an insect.

Marsupial A type of mammal that has a pouch where its newborn is fed and protected while it grows.

Molar tooth A strong, rounded tooth at the back of the mouth used for crushing food.

Nectar A sweet liquid produced by flowers to attract pollinators.

Nocturnal Active at night (compare to diurnal.)

Reptile

These cold-blooded creatures are covered in dry skin and scales. Their young hatch from eggs. Examples in this book: crocodile, snake, tortoise, chameleon, Komodo dragon.

Fish

These creatures live in the water; they have scales, fins, and breathe through gills. Examples in this book: seahorse, shark.

Amphibian

These cold-blooded creatures have gills and lungs for breathing. Their young live in the water and move onto land as adults. Most have slimy or sticky skin. Example in this book: frog.

Organ A part of the body with a particular job to do, such as the heart or brain.

Plankton Tiny plants and creatures that float in water; a major source of food for lots of animals.

Pollinator a creature such as an insect, bird, or bat that carries pollen from flower to flower to aid reproduction.

Predator A creature that hunts for food (known as its prey.)

Prehensile Able to grab or cling on, such as the tail of a seahorse or monkey.

Prey A creature that is eaten by another creature.

Sap A liquid in a plant that carries water and nutrients.

Social (insect) Living in an organized group, such as a colony of ants.

Spine The backbone, which protects the spinal cord and supports the body.

Teeth Animals have teeth to help them cut, grip, or grind food; there are three basic types (incisors, canines, molars.)

Tentacle A long, thin body part used for grabbing or feeding.

Toxic Producing a poison that is put into another animal by the victim biting the host.

Toxin A poisonous substance made by plants or animals.

Venomous Producing a poison that is put into another animal by the victim being bitten or stung.

Vertebrate A creature with a spine, such as the classes of animals above.

Wingspan The distance from the tip of a bird/bat's wing to the tip of its other wing.

Index